The Linnet's Wings

TO CATCH A FROG

Have you ever wished when fretting
'Bout the chilly air of spring,
When the days are longer getting
And the frogs begin to sing,
Have you ever wished that you could
Just change places with the frog—

Let him shoulder all your trouble
And then leave you on the log,
In the middle of the mill-pond,
Nothing in the world to do?
Have you wished you could change places,
You be frog and frog be you? ...

William Henry Dawson

THE LINNET'S WINGS

TAKE ALL MY LOVES

Sonnet 40: Take All My Loves My Love
by William Shakespeare

Take all my loves, my love, yea, take them all:
What hast thou then more than thou hadst before?
No love, my love, that thou mayst true love call—
All mine was thine before thou hadst this more.
Then if for my love thou my love receivest,
I cannot blame thee for my love thou usest;
But yet be blamed if thou this self deceivest
By wilful taste of what thyself refusest.
I do forgive thy robb'ry, gentle thief,
Although thou steal thee all my poverty;
And yet love knows it is a greater grief
To bear love's wrong than hate's known injury.
Lascivious grace, in whom all ill well shows,
Kill me with spites, yet we must not be foes.

Contributors

Barry Charman

Stephen Zelnic

Sean Farragher

Bill West

Bruce Harris

Tom Sheehan

Classic Yeats

Judith A Lawrence

Oonah V Joslin

RP Verlaine

Ann Egan

Miki Byrne

James G. Piatt

Ron. Lavalette

Dolores Duggan

Jan Wiezorek

Jo Ann Newton

Anne Donnellan

Art: Title, Blind Pew, Medium,
Watercolour on Card
Artist, MLF, © MLF 2019

In The Dock

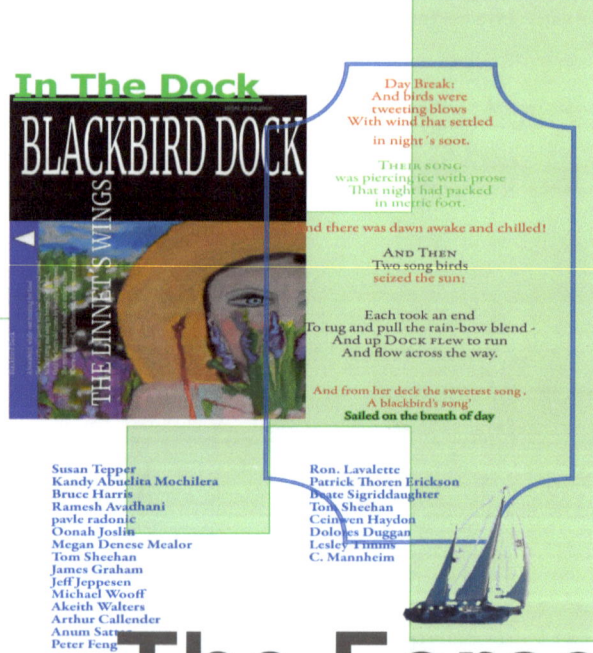

Day Break:
And birds were
tweeting blows
With wind that settled
in night's soot.

Their song
was piercing ice with prose
That night had packed
in metric foot.

And there was dawn awake and chilled!

And Then
Two song birds
seized the sun:

Each took an end
To tug and pull the rain-bow blend -
And up Dock flew to run
And flow across the way.

And from her deck the sweetest song,
A blackbird's song'
Sailed on the breath of day

Susan Tepper
Kandy Abuelita Mochilera
Bruce Harris
Ramesh Avadhani
pavle radonic
Oonah Joslin
Megan Denese Mealor
Tom Sheehan
James Graham
Jeff Jeppesen
Michael Wooff
Akeith Walters
Arthur Callender
Anum Sat
Peter Feng

Ron. Lavalette
Patrick Thoren Erickson
Beate Sigriddaughter
Tom Sheehan
Ceinwen Haydon
Dolores Duggan
Lesley Timms
C. Mannheim

Out Of The Cradle Endlessly Rocking
By Walt Whitman

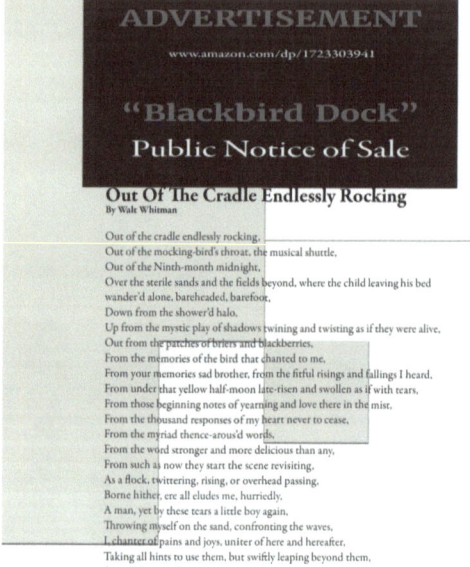

Out of the cradle endlessly rocking,
Out of the mocking-bird's throat, the musical shuttle,
Out of the Ninth-month midnight,
Over the sterile sands and the fields beyond, where the child leaving his bed
wander'd alone, bareheaded, barefoot,
Down from the shower'd halo,
Up from the mystic play of shadows twining and twisting as if they were alive,
Out from the patches of briers and blackberries,
From the memories of the bird that chanted to me,
From your memories sad brother, from the fitful risings and fallings I heard,
From under that yellow half-moon late-risen and swollen as if with tears,
From those beginning notes of yearning and love there in the mist,
From the thousand responses of my heart never to cease,
From the myriad thence-arous'd words,
From the word stronger and more delicious than any,
From such as now they start the scene revisiting,
As a flock, twittering, rising, or overhead passing,
Borne hither, ere all eludes me, hurriedly,
A man, yet by these tears a little boy again,
Throwing myself on the sand, confronting the waves,
I chanter of pains and joys, uniter of here and hereafter,
Taking all hints to use them, but swiftly leaping beyond them,
A reminiscence sing.

61

Leaves of Grass, Extract

The Force of Statistics

Taken from "Literary Lapses" by Stephen Leacock

They were sitting on a seat of the car, immediately in front of me. I was consequently able to hear all that they were saying. They were evidently strangers who had dropped into a conversation. They both had the air of men who considered themselves profoundly interesting as minds. It was plain that each laboured under the impression that he was a ripe thinker.

One had just been reading a book which lay in his lap.

"I've been reading some very interesting statistics," he was saying to the other thinker.

"Ah, statistics" said the other; "wonderful things, sir, statistics; very fond of them myself."

"I find, for instance," the first man went on, "that a drop of water is filled with little...with little...I forget just what

you call them...little—er—things, every cubic inch containing—er—containing...let me see..."

"Say a million," said the other thinker, encouragingly.

"Yes, a million, or possibly a billion...but at any rate, ever so many of them."

"Is it possible?" said the other. "But really, you know there are wonderful things in the world. Now, coal...take coal..."

"Very, good," said his friend, "let us take coal," settling back in his seat with the air of an intellect about to feed itself.

"Do you know that every ton of coal burnt in an engine will drag a train of cars as long as...I forget the exact length, but say a train of cars of such and such a length, and weighing, say so much...from...from...hum! for the moment the exact distance escapes me...drag it from..."

"From here to the moon," suggested the other.

"Ah, very likely; yes, from here to the moon. Wonderful, isn't it?"

"But the most stupendous calculation of all, sir, is in regard to the distance from the earth to the sun. Positively, sir, a cannon-ball—er—fired at the sun..."

"Fired at the sun," nodded the other, approvingly, as if he had often seen it done.

"And travelling at the rate of...of..."

"Of three cents a mile," hinted the listener.

"No, no, you misunderstand me,—but travelling at a fearful rate, simply fearful, sir, would take a hundred million—no, a hundred billion—in short would take a scandalously long time in getting there—"

At this point I could stand no more. I interrupted—"Provided it were fired from Philadelphia," I said, and passed into the smoking-car.

Funeral Symphony (I)

The Flowers
by Robert Louis Stevenson

All the names I know from nurse:
Gardener's garters, Shepherd's purse,
Bachelor's buttons, Lady's smock,
And the Lady Hollyhock.

Fairy places, fairy things,
Fairy woods where the wild bee wings,
Tiny trees for tiny dames--
These must all be fairy names!

Tiny woods below whose boughs
Shady fairies weave a house;
Tiny tree-tops, rose or thyme,
Where the braver fairies climb!

Fair are grown-up people's trees,
But the fairest woods are these;
Where, if I were not so tall,
I should live for good and all.

Funeral Symphony (II)

The Lanawn Shee
by Francis Ledwidge

Powdered and perfumed the full bee
Winged heavily across the clover,
And where the hills were dim with dew,
Purple and blue the west leaned over.

A willow spray dipped in the stream,
Moving a gleam of silver ringing,
And by a finny creek a maid
Filled all the shade with softest singing.

Funeral Symphony (II)
Mikalojus Konstantinas Ciurlionis
Date: 1903
Style: Symbolism
Series: Funeral Symphony
Genre: symbolic painting
Media: pastel, paper

Funeral Symphony (III)

Listening, my heart and soul at strife,
On the edge of life I seemed to hover,'
For I knew my love had come at last,
That my joy was past and my gladness over.

I tiptoed gently up and stooped
Above her looped and shining tresses,
And asked her of her kin and name,
And why she came from fairy places.

She told me of a sunny coast
Beyond the most adventurous sailor,
Where she had spent a thousand years
Out of the fears that now assail her.

And there, she told me, honey drops
Out of the tops of ash and willow,
And in the mellow shadow Sleep
Doth sweetly keep her poppy pillow.

Nor Autumn with her brown line marks
The time of larks, the length of roses,
But song-time there is over never
Nor flower-time ever, ever closes.

And wildly through uncurling ferns
Fast water turns down valleys singing,
Filling with scented winds the dales,
Setting the bells of sleep a-ringing.

Funeral Symphony (IV)

And when the thin moon lowly
sinks,Through cloudy chinks a silver glory
Lingers upon the left of night
Till dawn delights the meadows hoary.

And by the lakes the skies are white,
(Oh, the delight!) when swans are coming,
Among the flowers sweet joy-bells peal,
And quick bees wheel in drowsy humming

The squirrel leaves her dusty house
And in the boughs makes fearless gambol,
And, falling down in fire-drops, red,
The fruit is shed from every bramble.

Then, gathered all about the trees
Glad galaxies of youth are dancing,
Treading the perfume of the flowers,
Filling the hours with mazy glancing.

And when the dance is done, the trees
Are left to peace and the brown woodpecker,
And on the western slopes of sky
The day's blue eye begins to flicker.

But at the sighing of the leaves,
When all earth grieves for lights departed
An ancient and a sad desire
Steals in to tire the human-hearted.

No fairy aid can save them now
Nor turn their prow upon the ocean,
The hundred years that missed each heart
Above them start their wheels in motion.

And so our loves are lost, she sighed,
And far and wide we seek new treasure,
For who on Time or Timeless hills
Can live the ills of loveless leisure ?

Fairer than Usna's youngest son,
0, my poor one, what flower-bed holds you?
Or, wrecked upon the shores of home,
What wave of foam with white enfolds you ?

You rode with kings on hills of green,
And lovely queens have served you banquet,
Sweet wine from berries bruised they brought
And shyly sought the lips which drank it.

But in your dim grave of the sea
There shall not be a friend to love you.
And ever heedless of your loss
The earth ships cross the storms above you.

And still the chase goes on, and still
The wine shall spill, and vacant places
Be given over to the new
As love untrue keeps changing faces.

And I must wander with my song
Far from the young till love returning,
Brings me the beautiful reward
Of some heart stirred by my long yearning.

Friend, have you heard a bird lament
When sleet is sent for April weather ?
As beautiful she told her grief,
As down through leaf and flower I led her.

And friend, could I remain unstirred
Without a word for such a sorrow ?
Say, can the lark forget the cloud
When poppies shroud the seeded furrow ?

Like a poor widow whose late grief
Seeks for relief in lonely byeways,
The moon, companionless and dim,
Took her dull rim through starless highways.

I was too weak with dreams to feel
Enchantment steal with guilt upon me,
She slipped, a flower upon the wind,
And laughed to find how she had won me.

From hill to hill, from land to land,
Her lovely hand is beckoning for me,
I follow on through dangerous zones,
Cross dead men's bones and oceans stormy.

Some day I know she'll wait at last
And lock me fast in white embraces,
And down mysterious ways of love
We two shall move to fairy places.

Funeral Symphony (**V**)

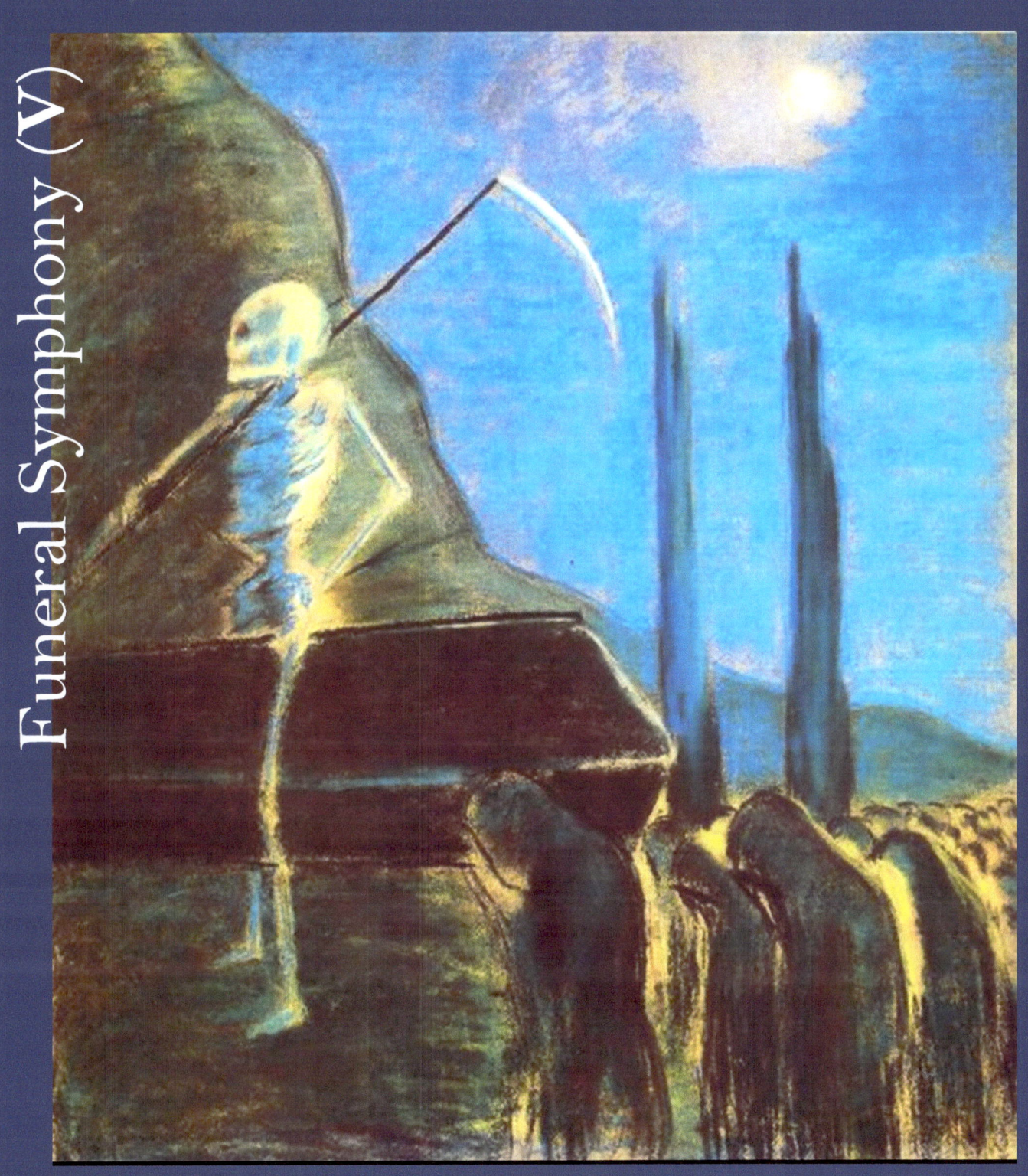

Mikalojus Konstantinas Ciurlionis, Date: 1903, Style: Symbolism, Series: Funeral Symphony, Genre: symbolic painting, Media: pastel, paper

Funeral Symphony (VI)

Funeral Symphony (VII)

Other Publications
"The Song of Hiawatha" by Henry Wadsworth Longfellow ISBN 1 3: 978-1 4801 76423- -
https://www.amazon.com/dp/1480176427

Chapbooks
"One Day Tells Its Tale to Another" by Nonnie Augustine ISBN-1 3: 978-1 4801 86354
https://www.amazon.com/dp/1482730995
"About the Weather-- Spring Trending" by Marie Lynam Fitzpatrick ISBN-1 3: 978-0993049330
"Disabled Monsters" by John C. Mannone ISBN-1 3:978-1 522869504
 https://www.amazon.com/dp/0993049389
"Three Pounds of Cells" by Oonah V Joslin ISBN-1 3: 978-0993049378
https://www.amazon.com/dp/0993049370

Poetry and Photography
"This Crazy Urge to Live" by Bobby Steve Baker ISBN-1 3: 978-099304909

Short Story Collections
"The Guy Thing" by Bruce Harris ISBN-1 3: 978-1 98111 6409
https://www.amazon.com/dp/1981116400

Poetry Series
Spring Poetry, 201 5 ISBN-1 3: 978-1 51 2051 225
https://www.amazon.com/dp/1512051225
Spring Poetry, "Ghosts," 201 6 ISBN-1 3: 978-1 51 7567637
 https://www.amazon.com/dp/1517567637
Autumn Poets, 201 5, ISBN-1 3: 978-1 51 91 57827
https://www.amazon.com/dp/1519157827
Autumn Poets,"There´s Magic in the Pictures" 201 6 ISBN-1 3: 978-1 537361 659
https://www.amazon.es/dp/1537361651
Summer Poets, 201 5 ISBN-1 3: 978-1 51 4761 71 7
https://www.amazon.com/dp/1514761718
Summer Poets, Just Like "Peer Gynt" ISBN-1 3: 978-1 53286511 4
https://www.amazon.com/dp/1 533245886

Christmas Series
The Linnet´s Wings: "A Christmas Canzonet" ISBN-1 3: 978-1 51 9581 686
https://www.amazon.com/dp/1519581688
The Linnet´s Wings: "A Christmas Canzonet" ISBN-1 3: 978-1 540454935
https://www.amazon.com/dp/1540454932
A Christmas Canzonet: "Dreamers" ISBN-1 3: 978-1 977809070
https://www.amazon.com/dp/1 977809073

Poem on the Wind: Art and Poetry Series
"Purple Kisses" by Priya Prithviraj ISBN-1 3: 978-1 978203266

For permission requests, mail the publisher at: thelinnetswings@gmail.com

ISBN: 978-1-9164622-6-7

 2020
First Edition May 2020

Book and Cover Design: Mari Fitzpatrick, 2020

Table of Contents

The Hay Wain by John Constable

"Je pense ...
À quiconque a perdu ce qui ne se retrouve
Jamais, jamais!"

(I think . . .
Of whomever has lost that which can
Never, never be found again!.)

Charles Baudelaire

PART ONE

"It's a dangerous business, Frodo, going out your door.
You step onto the road, and if you don't keep your feet,
there's no knowing where you might be swept off to."
— J.R.R. Tolkien, The Lord of the Rings

MID TONES

Dickens' Dream by Robert William Buss
Date: 1875, Style: Romanticism, Genre: genre painting

Turn the Page

Take a key, lock the door
there is nothing left to do
Walk away, don't look back
life is waiting ...

Go alone and have fun
life's too short to be undone
You know the way
it's yours for the taking

Life is good, love is kind
and it has you on its mind
You're a match for whatever
life is asking

to be happy is your lot
it's why you came here to this spot
It has beauty and has heart
life's breathtaking

Go alone and have fun
life's too short to be undone
Break the rules
write your own
Live the life you own

Turn the page, walk away
don't look back, own the day
It's there, and it's yours,

Stay away, don't go back
too much was said ...

Mari

[pic]

[This imposing statue in New York City's Central Park, shows Martí reeling from his mortal wounds. The Inscription reads: APOSTLE OF CUBAN INDEPENDENCE / LEADER OF THE PEOPLES OF AMERICA / AND DEFENDER OF HUMAN DIGNITY / HIS LITERARY GENIUS VIED WITH HIS / POLITICAL FORESIGHT. HE WAS BORN / IN HAVANA ON JANUARY 28, 1853 / FOR FIFTEEN YEARS OF HIS EXILE HE LIVED IN THE CITY OF NEW YORK. / HE DIED IN ACTION AT DOS RIOS IN / ORIENTE PROVINCE ON MAY 19, 1895.]

The Apostle: Cuba's Immortal José Martí

by

Stephen Zelnick

José Julián Martí Pérez (Cuban, 1853-1895) was aware he was the architect of a New World, a future he would never see. Like that dream-world, Martí came from nowhere. His father was from Valencia, a Spanish artilleryman; his mother from the Canary Islands. "Pepe" grew up in Havana in near poverty but found a teacher who cultivated his youthful idealism and patriotic fervor. At sixteen, Marti was publishing attacks advocating liberation from Spain. Arrested for disloyalty, he was sentenced to fifteen years at hard labor. Injured working, Martí was released and deported to Spain; he was lucky not to be executed. These years were tumultuous as Spain struggled between republicanism and devotion to a faded royalism. Its New World empire faced slave rebellion on the Caribbean sugar and tobacco plantations, bitter anger of the campesinos, and protests against Spain's harsh treatment of its rebellious empire.

Unable to return to Cuba, Martí lived in Mexico, Venezuela, Panama, and in Cuban exile communities in New York and Florida. There he envisioned a pan-Hispanic world, a new breed of person, hungry for liberation and respect, one with close bonds to family, neighbors, and the rural rhythms of nature.

The New World was ripe for revolution, and Spain was willing to inflict its miseries on its colonies. In the 1820s, Simon Bolivar, a Venezuelan, liberated several nations from Spanish control. For a time, France ruled Mexico, and native tribes challenged Spanish rule in what would become the US Southwest. In Cuba, decades later, Martí's contemporaries, vastly outnumbered and under-supplied, fought Spain to a standstill in a ten-year war (1868-78). And looming in wait stood the United States, hungry for conquest. When Martí died in battle in 1895 the Spanish-American War was three years off, but Martí judged the US a dangerous prospect for Central and Latin America, and the Caribbean island nations.

Martí was deeply influenced by Simon Bolivar. Bolivar, encouraged by Napoleon's successes, dedicated himself to building a vast independent republic, a "Gran Colombia". At its height it included Venezuela, Colombia, Panama, Ecuador, Bolivia, parts of northern Peru, western Guyana, and northwestern Brazil. The project collapsed in the early 1830s. Nonetheless, Bolivar liberated several nations from Spanish rule, freed the enslaved Africans and indigenous populations, and invited the subjects of Spanish colonialism to envision a confederation of nations. When Hugo Chavez and Fidel Castro lent encouragement to one another, they identified as Bolivarians. And Martí and Puerto Rico's Jose de Diego were energized by Bolivar's idea of uniting people who shared tribal origins, language, and the misery of Spanish colonialism, and who feared the prospect of Anglo rule.

[pic]

[Simon Bolivar hoped to construct a "Gran Colombia". When Fidel Castro and Hugo Chavez called themselves "Bolivarians", they were reviving this post-colonial vision of a world ruled by indigenous peoples, descendants of enslaved Africans and of mestizos, and children of Spain.]

1.

Martí was energized by his core belief in "Natural Man". Europe and the Anglos of "El Norte" trusted in elaborate learning over direct experience. Martí embraced transcendentalism and Rousseau's trust in those who embrace nature in work and life. On Emerson, he writes: "He was educated to teach a creed and returned his ministerial coat to the believers because he felt the august cloak of nature upon his shoulders. He followed no system, for that struck him as the act of a blind man or a servant; he believed in no system, for that struck him as the act of a weak, low, and envious mind. He plunged into nature and emerged from her radiant." For Martí the Indian of the American forests knows nature and his own nature on his skin and in his bones. He distinguishes lies from truth, whereas for the urban, civilized person all is negotiable in the garb of success and the play of language. Hard work unites persons who would be free and loving: "Work makes men beautiful. The sight of a field hand, an ironworker, or a sailor is rejuvenating. As they grapple with nature's forces, they come to be as fair as nature."

[Ralph Waldo Emerson, 1803-1882, leading voice of the transcendentalist movement in the United States influenced Martí with his ideas of radical liberty and breaking loose from the past: "Do not go where the path may lead, go instead where there is no path and leave a trail."]

America suffers from the burden of Europe, its class distinctions, racism, and luxury. Like the prophet Isaiah, Marti condemned high culture's arrogance and refinement, especially in those of the New World who preserve the old: Those with "their puny arms, with bracelets and painted nails, the arms of Madrid or of Paris ... These sons of carpenters who are ashamed that their father was a carpenter! These men born in America who are ashamed of the mother who raised them because she wears an Indian apron ...." In his masterpiece, "Our America," Martí declares war on the false learning imported from Europe: "In America the natural man has triumphed over the imported books. Natural men have triumphed over an artificial intelligentsia. The native mestizo has triumphed over the alien, pure-blooded criollo. The battle is not between civilization and barbarity, but between false erudition and nature."

[pic]

[Walt Whitman, 1819-1892, liberated poetry from its classical restraints and incorporated all aspects of society and of nature. Spanish poetry in particular was bound by tradition in its subject matter, vocabulary, and techniques. Martí took a path different from Whitman's, working in compressed and tight-packed forms instead of Whitman's open lines.]

Martí saw an America built on democracy, on mutual respect and affection, hard work and kindness and fellow feeling. This is not a poetic dream, but the root of any successful political arrangement: "To govern well, one must attend well to the reality of the place that is governed. In America, the good ruler does not need to know how the German or the Frenchman is governed, but what elements his own country is composed of and how he can marshal them so as to reach, by means and institutions born from the country itself, the desirable state in which every man knows himself and is active, and all men enjoy the abundance that Nature, for good of all, has bestowed on the country they make fruitful by their labor and defend with their lives." Martí's goal is the renovation of human possibility offered by America. He envisions a Hispanic world, freed from Spain, and absorbing strength from indigenous peoples, small farmers and farmworkers, and enslaved Africans who yearn for freedom and fellowship. All this requires a different political science: "Politics is strategy. Nations must continually criticize themselves, for criticism is health, but with a single heart and a single mind. Lower yourselves to the unfortunate and raise them up in your arms! Let the heart's fires unfreeze all that is motionless in America; and let the country's natural blood surge and throb through its veins! Standing tall, the workman's eyes full of joy, the new men of America are saluting each other from one country to another. Natural statesmen are emerging from the direct study of nature; they read in order to apply what they read, not copy it."

Martí mocks the colonial world: "What a vision we were: the chest of an athlete, the hands of a dandy, and the forehead of a child. We were a whole fancy dress ball, in English trousers, a Parisian waistcoat, a North American overcoat, and a Spanish bullfighter's hat. The Indian circled about us, mute, and went to the mountaintop to christen his children. The black, pursued from afar, alone and unknown, sang his heart's music in the night, between waves and wild beasts. The campesinos, the men of the land, the creators, rose up in blind indignation against the disdainful city, their own creation. We wore epaulets and judge's robes, in countries that came into the world wearing rope sandals and Indian headbands."

[pic]

[This bit of cigar box art illustrates Martí's mockery. An Indian, clutching tobacco leaves joins a daughter of Spain, bearing heraldry, and both blessed with justice and a freer style by the spirit of a New Cuba.]

In his call for armed struggle against the past, Martí sees bold possibilities. In "To Cuba!" he is filled with both indignation and hope for a war against empire: "We must cast into the fire—for its impurity and uselessness—the silken hand that, by way of greeting, licks the bloodied, debased hand of its country's corrupter, and instead beckon the rough hand that works the rifle which must drive the insolent to the sea, and the saintly hand, sometimes bony from hunger, that caresses and constructs in darkness, with the hope of the humble, the just and the warmhearted patria, that will rise from the sea to skies with arms open to all mankind." In his "Montecristi Manifesto", Martí foresees: "A free nation, where work is open to all, positioned at the very mouth of the rich and industrial universe, [that] will without obstacle and with some advantage replace, after a war inspired by the purest self-sacrifice and carried out in keeping with it, the shameful nation where well-being is obtained only in exchange for an express or tacit complicity with the tyranny of the grasping foreigners who bleed and corrupt it."

[pic]

[This dream-world vision of a Cuban "central", depicts a pleasant, well-ordered, and humane community, all working to the same end, rendering cane into sugar, and sharing work and wealth.]

[pic]

[The real world of cutting and gathering cane.]

2.

Famed as a liberator, Martí is famed, too, as a poet. Less well known is his journalism, raucous and engaged, with speed and point, dramatizing the United States and its tawdry circus. Following Carlyle's style, Martí motivates his prose with dizzying references, a riot of verbs, compression, sentences broken into particles in motion. Looking forward, Martí is John Dos Passos, Tom Wolfe, Hunter S. Thompson, rushing to snap a photo of the diversity and frenzied energies of the United States. Martí lived in the US for fifteen years and loved and hated it. He adored the idyll of small towns, farms and woodland, and tight-knit communities; and Martí could not resist the turbulence and danger of the northern cities.

In 1881, Charles Guiteau shot President James Garfield, recently elected President. Popular, even beloved, Garfield died some months later, and the trial of Guiteau, obviously deranged, offered a bizarre spectacle. Martí takes us there:

the public: curious, laughing, profane, which, as if watching the convulsions of a drunken animal, rejoices in the spasms, outbursts, jeers, cynical jokes, and brutal gestures of the accused. The onlookers rock with gales of laughter; the prisoner shares in the laughter he provokes; the ushers call for silence; and the judge scolds in vain. The mournful ghost of the venerated victim does not come to trouble the merriment of the room.

The rhythm and pacing of this passage demonstrate poetic attentiveness, as the two sentences unwind, from staccato items, to precise balance, and to a peculiar reflection of incongruity, implicating "mournful" with "merriment".

Or consider this brilliant passage from "Prizefight", an effort to render the crazed spirit of the monstrosity of the North:

I can still see the street urchins, who are like green fruit that has rotted on the vine, hanging from the wheels and windows of the newspaper wagon, as if a beehive had been knocked over. A horde of buyers waits around the wagon, which the dray horse is already pulling away, while the children go scrabbling along the ground among heaps of newspapers: wretched little girls in rags, well-dressed lasses, whose fine garments lay bare their souls, and rapacious Irish lads who curse as they retrieve their tattered hats, fallen off in the scuffle, from the mud. And new wagons pull in, and new scufflings ensue.

The speed in the passage renders the chaos of the scene; the spectators eye whips from one event to the next the vocabulary rich in suggestion – "green fruit ... rotted on the vine"; "the children scrabbling ... among heaps"; "lasses, whose fine garments lay bare their souls"; "rapacious Irish lads ... tattered hats ... scufflings" – this is the art of a gifted word-smith.

[pic]

[Martí was uncomfortable with the crush of humanity in New York's tenement ghettoes.]

In "Inauguration Day", it doesn't take much to mistake Martí for Dickens:

The trains arrive, a flag in every window, loaded with Californians in felt hats who've come all the way from the Pacific Coast; the Sioux people, who have left its cars littered with corn husks; Texan cowboys, dressed in leather shirts, fringed pants, and broad-brimmed hats; Arkansas mountain men in calico dusters, their hats adorned with deer tails. Where will this mass of fanatics, pugilists, politicians, job-seekers, gawkers, peddlers, vagabonds, and thieves find lodging? In chairs, because there are no beds; on warped boards placed on top of bathtubs; against some counter with their heads on their arms, asleep over their whiskey with milk; on a visit to a house of ill-repute, where the girls are showing off the new outfits they wear when a President takes office for the first time; or walking, walking across the sticky asphalt with mud up to their ankles, water in their hearts, their suitcases mauled, their notebooks destroyed ...

The details, rushing by quickly, are compressed, with photographic precision – "Arkansas Mountain men in calico dusters" – and musical, lyrical charm. And, then, the energy of lists, hodge-podge "fanatics, pugilists, politicians ... peddlers, vagabonds, and thieves." The comic notion of Inaugural finery in the brothels; and the bedraggled journalists "their notebooks destroyed" is first-class Dos Passos.

In "The Truth About the United States", Martí analyzes a disease:

The hills of the Dakotas, and the barbarous virile nation that is arising there, are world's away from the leisured, privileged, class-bound, lustful, and unjust cities of the East. There is a whole world between the North of Schenectady, with its brick houses and lordly freedom, and the South of St. Petersburg, between the clean, self-interested town of the North and the loafers sitting on cracker barrels at the country store in the angry, impoverished, ramshackle, bitter gray towns of the South. An honorable man cannot help but observe that not only have the elements of diverse origin and tendency from which the United States was created failed, in three centuries of shared life and one century of political control, to merge, but their forced co-existence is exacerbating and accentuating their primary differences and transforming the unnatural federation into a harsh state of violent conquest."

We sweep the continent, with various details as in, "the clean, self-interested town of the North" – who expects "self-interested"? – and the cracker barrel, "bitter gray towns of the South." Martí's judgment is harsh and prescient, tracing the "state of violent conquest" to the "unnatural federation", often the pride and here the cause of the northern behemoth's failed ideals.

3.

Along with his journalism, Martí (1) authored political manifestoes, (2) raised funds throughout Latin America for wars of resistance against Spain, (3) wrote children's books, while imagining new models of education, (4) directed the Cuban Revolutionary Party, and also (5) wrote Spanish poetry in a new voice. The false grandeur of Spain belonged to a putrefying empire a world away. That silken world – puny, arrogant, and racist -- had nothing to offer the New World. American transcendentalism was rarefied and beyond the reach of the untutored. Whitman had a profound impact on New World poetry, but Marti aimed for something more compressed, more lyrical, forceful and spare.

[pic]

[Martí published only one book of poetry, Versos Sencillos (Simple Verses –1891); his second collection, Versos Libres (Free Verses – 1913) was gleaned from manuscripts and earlier publication. The 46 poems of Versos sencillos vary in topic and feeling, but they share a direct personal expression, unadorned, and in familiar lyrical form and basic vocabulary. Many have mistaken them as poetry for children.]

Some of his loveliest pieces are moral lessons. Martí wants a revolution free from violent emotions and vengeful passions. He fears the tendency of revolutionaries to raise themselves on heroic pedestals, dazzled by personal ambitions, and isolated from comrades.

Cultivo una rosa blanca,	I grow a white rose
En julio como en enero,	in July as in January,
Para el amigo sincero	for any honest friend
Que me da su mano franca.	who offers me his hand freely.
Y para el cruel que me arranca	And, for the cruel one
El corazón con que vivo,	who tears out my very heart,
Cardo ni oruga cultivo:	I cultivate neither thistle nor pest:
Cultivo la rosa blanca.	I grow the white rose for him, too.

The simple language and form of this stark lesson belies its moral complexity. The word "arranca" is strong; the harshness of "cardo" and "oruga" (caterpillar) is balanced by "la rosa blanca". The lesson contradicts our nature; our need to revenge an injury. To build a new society people who have fought against one another will need to be brothers and sisters working towards peace and cooperation. The red rose is passionate and bloody; the white rose peaceful and serene. The maxim is put in simple terms, no need to make the case.

[pic]

[Contemporary Black and White photos make Martí, with his prominent moustache, resemble a comic film actor from the 1920's. This painting gives us the thoughtful artist who wrote so well.]

Yo que vivo, aunque me he muerto,
Soy un gran descubridor,
Porque anoche he descubierto
La medicina de amor.

I who live, though I have died,
I am a great discoverer,
For last night I discovered
The medicine of love.

Cuando al peso de la cruz
El hombre morir resuelve,
Sale a hacer bien, lo hace, y vuelve
Como de un baño de luz.

When to bear the weight of the cross
a man resolves to die, he goes out
to do good, does it, and returns,
 bathed in light.

Martí was killed in his first military engagement, shot as he rushed on horseback into an ambush by Spanish troops. In several of his poems, he seems to predict his death and to think about what it will mean. Martí's use of Christian images is unusual; and invoking the "gran descubridor", makes the speaker Columbus venturing the world beyond. Can there be a medicine to death? The second stanza settles the paradox. The weight of the cross is the burden to liberate humankind from its colonial captivity. Those committed to the task earn forgiveness and rebirth

Yo no puedo olvidar nunca
La mañanita de otoño
En que le salió un retoño
A la pobre rama trunca.

I cannot forget
that autumn morn
when a bud sprouted
On a withered branch.

La mañanita en que, en vano,
Junto a la estufa apagada,
Una niña enamorada
Le tendió al viejo la mano.

The morn when, in vain,
near a cold stove
A loving girl
Reached for an old man's hand.

In this translation, I set out to compress an already terse poem. Martí squeezes his line hard, aiming at simplicity. The ideas and feeling in the poem are not simple; Recall Shakespeare's Sonnet 73, where song from an autumnal branch persists in memory, and passion from ashes. The poem compares two unrelated moments, challenging us to connect them; and then, with the link discovered, to make sense of "in vain". Does life renew? For the girl? For the old man? For both, for neither? The shadow cast by these questions leaves us aware of our spark of hope against the shadow of despair. Each stanza contains twenty words – so much from so little – for a poem that expands in imagination and emotion.

Si ves un monte de espumas,	Spot a mountain of mists,
Es mi verso lo que ves,	It's my verse you see,
Mi verso es un monte, y es	My verse a mountain, and
Un abanico de plumas.	A fan made of feathers.
Mi verso es como un puñal	My verse is like a dagger, from
Que por el puño echa flor:	each wound blooms a flower:
Mi verso es un surtidor	a fountain from which
Que da un agua de coral.	coral water flows.
Mi verso es de un verde claro	My verse is clear green
Y de un carmín encendido:	and burning red:
Mi verso es un ciervo herido	a wounded deer seeking
Que busca en el monte amparo.	refuge in the mountains.
Mi verso al valiente agrada:	My verse pleases the valiant:
Mi verso, breve y sincero,	Short and sweet, with
Es del vigor del acero	the strength of steel
Conque se funde la espada.	swords are made of.

Several of Martí's poems address his objectives in poetry. This explores contrasts – solid mountains against fragile fans and mists; daggers and flowers; cool and fiery colors, and retreats into pain; verse and swords. The "wounded deer" is the standard, where the poet eases love's injuries; but Martí poems are weapons to free readers from ignorance and the pain of subjection.

[pic]

[In 1896 Spanish General Valeriano Weyler introduced concentration camps to restrain Cubans in the countryside from assisting insurgent fighters. Thousands, mostly women and children, died of starvation and disease. He injured the Spanish cause by arousing the sentiments of the US public to intervene.]

4.

Versos Sinceros includes also stark narratives, brief and unpoetical, with Martí's characteristic compression and force.

El enemigo brutal	The brutal enemy
Nos pone fuego a la casa:	torched our house:
El sable la calle arrasa,	His sabre swept the street,
A la luna tropical.	Under the tropical moon.

Pocos salieron ilesos	Few escaped the
Del sable del español:	Spanish sabre unharmed: :
La calle, al salir el sol,	The street, at daybreak,
Era un reguero de sesos.	Was a trail of bloody brains.

Pasa, entre balas, un coche:	A coach passes, bullets flying:
Entran, llorando, a una muerta:	people enter, weeping, with a dead woman:
Llama una mano a la puerta	A hand knocks at the door
En lo negro de la noche.	In the dark night.

No hay bala que no taladre	Bullets drill into
El portón: y la mujer	the door: the woman who
Que llama, me ha dado el ser:	calls out, is she who gave me life:
Me viene a buscar mi madre.	My mother comes looking for me.

A la boca de la muerte,	Seeks me at the mouth of death,
Los valientes habaneros	and the valiant Havanans
Se quitaron los sombreros	removed their sombreros
Ante la matrona fuerte.	Before this powerful matron.

Y después que nos besamos	And afterwards, we kissed
Como dos locos, me dijo:	like two lunatics, and she said to me:
«¡Vamos pronto, vamos, hijo:	"We're going son, let's go:
La niña está sola: vamos!».	The little one, she's all alone: let's go!"

Events fly past, chaos and fright, quick snapshots, etched in few words. Some are long views; others painfully local; the house aflame under the tropical moon. The street mucked up with brains and blood; a carriage rushing passed, a frantic knock, a dead woman, bullets flying – the reader is thrust into the boy's nightmare.

And then rescue, and Havanan soldiers, in awe at his mother's courage. The quick embrace, and more work to do, and the unadorned "vamos, hijo" – no time for speeches – the boy is self-involved, understandingly, but the mother has another little one to rescue. Scene action, character, emotion – all in a tight space, each line drawn deftly, each detail precise and economical – this is the horror of the helpless caught in war's frenzy, even the "valiant Havanans" doing their best against the Spanish sword that knows no mercy.

[pic]

[Throughout the century, Cubans battled the Spanish and local plantation owners.]

El rayo surca, sangriento,
El lóbrego nubarrón:
Echa el barco, ciento a ciento,
Los negros por el portón.

An angry ray pierces
the bloodstained storm cloud:
as the ship pours out her Negroes,
by the hundreds at the gate.

El viento, fiero, quebraba
Los almácigos copudos;
Andaba la hilera, andaba,
De los esclavos desnudos.

A fierce wind pounds
the dense trees of the plantations;
as naked slaves, one after another,
Slowly file by.

El temporal sacudía
Los barracones henchidos:
Una madre con su cría
Pasaba, dando alaridos.

The wild storm shook
the crowded barracoons:
A mother with her infant,
Passed by, howling.

Rojo, como en el desierto,
Salió el sol al horizonte:
Y alumbró a un esclavo muerto,
Colgado a un seibo del monte.

Red, as in the desert,
rose the sun at the horizon:
and lit up the body of a dead slave
hanging from a ceiba tree on the mountain.

Un niño lo vio: tembló
De pasión por los que gimen:
¡Y, al pie del muerto, juró
lavar con su vida el crimen!

A boy saw it and trembled
from passion for all who groan:
And, at the foot of the dead man, swore
To avenge the crime with his life!

This narrative includes five brief moments. The ship disgorging its human cargo, the dispirited procession, a mother with the screaming infant, the lynching on the mountainside ... the boy's reaction and oath of vengeance. The scenes link heaven and earth, in a vast theater of brutality – the piercing ray, fierce wind, wild storm, and angry morning light – each brings violence. The poet's voice is restrained. The boy's resolve needs no rhetoric – spare and definite as the heavens.

[pic]

[With the rebellions in Haiti and Dominica, Cuba's sugar plantations prospered and became the prime destination for enslaved Africans. Between 1790 and 1820, 350,000 Africans arrived in Cuba, nearly equaling the native population. In 1868 rebellion erupted, which led to a ten-year war. Legal emancipation was set in motion but was not completed until 1886.]

[pic]

[Mexican Diego Rivera, "Sugar Cane" portrays the machine efficiency in producing this high value crop. Cane cutters bend in unison, while others tie and carry the heavy stalks. An overseer drives them with whip and pistol, while a black guard looks on, armed for trouble. On the verandah, a blond-haired fellow, done in by the heat, rests in a hammock.

Por tus ojos encendidos
Y lo mal puesto de un broche,
Pensé que estuviste anoche
Jugando a juegos prohibidos.

From your redened eyes
and your clasp pinned awry,
I thought you spent last night
Playing dirty games.

Te odié por vil y alevosa:
Te odié con odio de muerte:
Náusea me daba de verte
Tan villana y tan hermosa.

For being vile and devious
I despised you with deadly hatred:
Just seeing you nauseated me,
So villainous, yet so beautiful.

Y por la esquela que vi
Sin saber cómo ni cuándo,
Sé que estuviste llorando
Toda la noche por mí.

Then from the death notice I saw,
Not telling how or when,
I knew you had been weeping
All night for me.

This little drama of doubt in love is direct and chilling – "Just seeing you nauseated me" – and quick to resolution. He has mistaken her appearance totally, assuming "juegos prohibidos", on the flimsiest evidence, while she has been grieving for him. Where do such evil thoughts come from? What's wrong with us, lost in the labyrinth of fear and distrust? The poem is quick, like mistaken surmises, confirmed by nothing and tearing at our inner composure.

El alma trémula y sola	My soul, trembling and alone,
Padece al anochecer:	suffers at dusk:
Hay baile; vamos a ver	There's dancing; let's go see
La bailarina española.	The Spanish dancer.
Han hecho bien en quitar	It's good they've got rid of
El banderón de la acera;	the sidewalk banner;
Porque si está la bandera,	were the flag there, I don't know
No sé, yo no puedo entrar.	if I could enter.
Ya llega la bailarina:	the dancer comes on:
Soberbia y pálida llega;	Proud and pale;
¿Cómo dicen que es gallega?	How can they say she's Galician?
Pues dicen mal: es divina.	They're so wrong: she's divine.
Lleva un sombrero torero	She wears a toreador's hat
Y una capa carmesí:	and a carmine cape:
¡Lo mismo que un alelí	She's put a carnation
Que se pusiera un sombrero!	in her hat!
Se ve, de paso, la ceja,	As she passes by, one sees her eyebrow,
Ceja de mora traidora:	the eyebrow of a treacherous Moor
Y la mirada, de mora:	And the look, that Moorish look:
Y como nieve la oreja.	While her ear is white as snow.
Preludian, bajan la luz,	The introduction sounds, the light dims,
Y sale en bata y mantón,	she comes, in gown and cape,
La virgen de la Asunción	a virgin of the Assumption,
Bailando un baile andaluz.	Dancing an Andalusian dance.
Alza, retando, la frente;	She lifts her head in challenge;
Crúzase al hombro la manta:	throws her shawl over her shoulder:
En arco el brazo levanta:	Raises her arm in an arc:
Mueve despacio el pie ardiente.	Moves slowly her tapping foot.
Repica con los tacones	Then stamps her heels
El tablado zalamera,	battering the floorboards,

18

Como si la tabla fuera	as if the planks were
Tablado de corazones.	Made of lovers' hearts.
Y va el convite creciendo	So goes her beckoning, rising
En las llamas de los ojos,	in the fire of her eyes,
Y el manto de flecos rojos	as her red-flecked cape
Se va en el aire meciendo.	Rends the air.
Súbito, de un salto arranca:	Suddenly, a wild leap:
Húrtase, se quiebra, gira:	She stops, turns away, turns back:
Abre en dos la cachemira,	Parts her cashmere cloak, and
Ofrece la bata blanca.	Reveals her white sheath.
El cuerpo cede y ondea;	Her body yields and undulates;
La boca abierta provoca;	her open mouth provokes:
Es una rosa la boca;	A rose in her mouth; as
Lentamente taconea.	Slowly she taps.
Recoge, de un débil giro,	She gathers, with a slight flourish,
El manto de flecos rojos:	her red flecked cape:
Se va, cerrando los ojos,	she's gone, closing her eyes,
Se va, como en un suspiro...	gone, moving like a sigh....
Baila muy bien la española,	How well the Spanish girl dances,
Es blanco y rojo el mantón:	with cloak both white and red:
¡Vuelve, fosca, a un rincón	Returning, spent, to my little cell
El alma trémula y sola!	My soul trembles, all alone!

[pic]

Martí writes of sexual temptation and of taming desire. Spain gave the New World its language and codes of courtesy, and also the passionate song and dance of flamenco, with delights offered and artfully withheld. The speaker is uneasy entering the premises. The dancer has that dark enticing, Moorish look, the arched, too knowing eyebrow, but also hints of virginity in the whiteness of her delicate ear. Perhaps he can imagine she is the Virgin of the Assumption, dancing a folkdance.

But her dancing is wild -- welcoming, teasing, and denying -- mocking the conventional lyricism of love. She beckons the speaker, invites him to possess her, turns away, and turning back reveals her body sheathed in a tight-fitted gown. She "undulates", yields and provokes, but then recedes into her own dream of passion fulfilled, moving like a sigh. Translators find "spent" (fosca) too explicit as the viewer's sexual exhaustion, answering the dancer's self-obliterating descent into her private rapture.

Yo visitaré anhelante	I will visit longingly
Los rincones donde a solas	the places we were
Estuvimos yo y mi amante	alone, I and my dear one,
Retozando con las olas.	Frolicking with the waves.
Solos los dos estuvimos,	Alone the two of us,
Solos, con la compañía	alone, along with
De dos pájaros que vimos	two birds we saw
Meterse en la gruta umbría.	Entering a secluded cave.
Y ella, clavando los ojos,	And she, fixing her eyes,
En la pareja ligera,	on the delicate pair,
Deshizo los lirios rojos	plucked at the red lillies
Que le dio la jardinera.	The gardener gave her.
La madreselva olorosa	The sweet-smelling honeysuckle
Cogió con sus manos ella,	she herself gathered,
Y una madama graciosa,	and a gracious "mademoiselle",
Y un jazmín como una estrella.	And a jasmin like a star.
Yo quise, diestro y galán,	Like a skillful gallant, I offered
Abrirle su quitasol;	to open her parasol;
Y ella me dijo: «¡Qué afán!	And she said to me: "what's the hurry!
¡Si hoy me gusta ver el sol!	Today I want to see the sun!"
»Nunca más altos he visto	"I have never seen oak trees
Estos nobles robledales:	higher than these:
Aquí debe estar el Cristo,	Christ must be here;
Porque están las catedrales.	They form cathedrals.
»Ya sé dónde ha de venir	"Now I know where my little girl
Mi niña a la comunión;	will come for her communion;
De blanco la he de vestir	I will dress her in white
Con un gran sombrero alón».	With a wide-brimmed hat."
Después, del calor al peso,	Later, oppressed by the heat,
Entramos por el camino,	we walked on,
Y nos dábamos un beso	and we kissed
En cuanto sonaba un trino.	As each trill sounded.

20

¡Volveré, cual quien no existe,	I will return, now that she's gone,
Al lago mudo y helado:	to that mute and icy lake;
Clavaré la quilla triste:	I will beach the sad keel;
Posaré el remo callado!	Set down the silent oar!

This last is more conventional. Young love, natural joy, birds and flowers, vast trees forming cathedral arches, intimacy and spontaneous kisses, and the heart prompted to imagine a future rich with promise – endling in loneliness, silence, and deep sadness, as death and separation end the journey.

As with other of Marti's tight-woven narrative poems, the lines are short and quick, glimpses, snapshots, a fleeting memory held by few words, an image or two. The speaker recalls a perfect day of sweetness and calm. The woman risks the sun and ventures a blissful vision of life's promise, a daughter prepared for communion in a natural cathedral of peace and eternal renewal.

The final stanza returns to the first and the promise of visiting the past. The frolicking waves are now a "mute and icy lake", unmoving and frozen in time and promise. Now she's gone, there is no future and no birds sing; nothing but the silent oar set down, the journey over. It's an achieved poem built with control and precision, the lines slow and easy in memory, and the sad conclusion rendered quietly, without protest – a mute acceptance of loss. And all accomplished in so few words.

[pic]

Jose Martí, Selected Writings, Penguin Classics, 2002. Ed. and Trans. Esther Allen. The source for the quoted journalism of Martí.

The poetry translations are my own, abandoning the meter and rhyme of most translations, in an attempt to reflect Martí's sharp eye and intense compression.

Stephen Zelnick, Professor Emeritus, Temple Univeristy
Loiza, Puerto Rico
November 2019

Continued fron P. 21
The Apostle: Page numbers and citations … with quotation

Pg. 5 … emerged from her radiant" (p. 19). From "Emerson", in Jose Marti: Selected Writings, Trans. Esther Allen.

Pg. 5 … as fair as nature" (p. 131), "Tributes to Marx".

Pg. 5 … an Indian apron" (p. 289), "Our America".

Pg. 5 … false erudition and nature" (p, 290).   [given in text]

Pg. 6 ... to defend with their lives" (p. 290), "Our America".

Pg. 6 … to apply what they read, not copy it" (p. 294), "Our America".

Pg. 6 … and Indian headbands" (p. 247), "Inauguration Day".

Pg. 7 … open to all mankind" (p. 131).   [given in text]

Pg. 7 … bleed and corrupt it" (p. 340).   [given in text]

Pg. 8 … merriment in the room" (p. 97), "The Trial of Guiteau".

Pg. 8 … new scufflings ensue" (p. 108), "Prizefight".

Pg. 9 … their notebooks destroyed" (p. 245), "Inauguration Day".

Pg. 10 … state of violent conquest" (p. 330), "The Truth about the United States".

And watch the rapids blast right past
The rolling tumbleweed that teems.
Where folk wear lively masks, to hide

From old considered tasks where thoughts
Are threaded through wild scapes
Made from cloth and fixed as window drapes
Then hung in rooms without a view

To stop good folk
 from seeing through

In the land of Flabbergast
it's browsers' job to stoke the themes,
To point the view will might typecast;
A voice, a stand, a stance, a scream!

Iambs cut through new moon beams
Their molds make good snug sleep-casts.
To drop beat-sheets down into dreams
So folk can follow glitter paths

miscellany drabble

Breton girl spinning by Paul Gauguin

Elephant
Franz Marc
Date: 1907
Style: Post-Impressionism
Genre: sketch and study
Media: chalk, paper

Cordeville by
Vincent van Gogh

The Corkers

Blitzy blotty fibberty flops
Snaggered passed the chimley plots
On bossy clouds in sparking flight
They flibped and blitzed the nightly blite

Small shiney specks shung in the sky
Nhivery slivers of moospies
Splopped down on earth in giffey reels
Reporting on the squaffling speils

"Let's smlash the blighters," said the 'pant
"we'll spull them down, let's make a plan."

S'off to work with paper trowls
They plaited blinders for the clan.
And splanted them with yeowling howls

That tripped up ladders to the sky
And scared the floppies way up high

O dear O sigh
when caught

The blitzy blotty fipperty 'pies
Just waved bye bye

Bisection Class

By Sam Hartburn

Barney trudged along the corridor, trying to delay the moment at which he would have to enter the classroom. He heard rapid footsteps behind as Tom and Sally rushed past, clearly eager to get to work. Barney suppressed a sigh as he approached the door, pushed it open and went to his desk.

He could hardly bear the thought of what lay ahead. The cruelty. Why were school children expected to cut up and torture innocents? Barbaric, that's what it was. Tom and Sally already had their instruments lined up on their desks, points sharpened, ready for action.

Mrs Donnelley swept into the classroom, a pile of A4 paper in her arms. Without even pausing to say hello she started to hand the papers out. "Bisection today," she said, as she marched round the room. "Per-pen-dic-u-lar. And don't look so doleful, Barney. A bit of compass work never hurt anybody."

Barney stared down at his desk. It might not have hurt anybody, but that didn't stop it hurting anything. The paper on his desk was empty save for one straight line across the centre. Perpendicular bisection. As far as Barney was concerned, one of the nastiest concepts ever imagined.

Tom and Sally were busy already, gleefully jabbing their compasses into the paper and drawing their arcs. Barney slowly picked up his compass and checked the point. Was it better to have it sharp for a clean cut? Or could he get away without piercing if it was blunt? Probably didn't make a difference either way. He eased the point into the paper at the end of the line, trying to leave a small gap so that it didn't actually touch the line. It didn't work. As the point went in he heard the scream.

Almost nothing compares to the scream of a line being pierced by a compass. Imagine a room full of hungry newborn babies crying at the top of their lungs, accompanied by a gang of seagulls fighting over a dropped chip, and you still don't even come close. That's what Barney thought, anyway. He clamped one hand over his ear and attempted to block the other with his elbow without dropping the compass, still surprised after all this time that nobody else seemed to hear it.

When the screaming had subsided, Barney drew his small arcs, one on either side of the line. That part wasn't so bad. After the initial piercing the line had taken up a steady moan and didn't seem to notice. It was worse when a line saw the arcs and realised what was coming. Barney took a deep breath and steeled himself to do the same thing on the other side. There was another scream as the point went in. Barney quickly drew his second set of arcs, crossing over the first set, and whipped the compass away.

The worst was still to come. Two points of intersection, one on each side of the line. It could only mean one thing. Barney picked up his ruler and twirled it between his fingers, putting off the inevitable. He glanced round the room and noticed a big pile of papers on Tom's desk. He must have done ten, maybe fifteen. It just didn't bear thinking about.

Barney returned his gaze to his own line, which had stopped moaning and was now letting out the occasional quiet sob. He placed his ruler on the intersection points, lined up his pencil, closed his eyes and, as fast as he could, ran the pencil down the ruler. There was a blood-curdling scream, then silence. One more line, gone. Bisected.

***

ART
Transverse Line, Wassily Kandinsky, Date: 1923; Alten / Dessau-alten, Germany, Style: Abstract Art, Genre: abstract, Media: oil, canvas

162 МОРОЗКО И ПАДЧЕРИЦА
Иллюстрация к русской народной сказке «Морозко». 1932

Head of the Family

by Bill West

It was the duvet sliding to the floor that woke me -- that and the smell of pipe tobacco.

To see one's dead father is always shocking. To see his disembodied head, topped with a sailor's cap, bobbing over your king-size bed is alarming in the extreme. And to see that bodiless head smoking a pipe, a rather fine briar with a rosewood bowl, if I'm not mistaken, possibly the one I bought him for his sixty-fourth birthday, is taking the whole nightmare business too far.

"Is that you?" I asked, my voice unsurprisingly thin.

He didn't seem to notice me at all. His head just floated up and down with that gentle rhythm associated with breathing in a person blessed with body parts.

It unnerved me that the silky trails of smoke seemed real, had greater density than his flesh. Did that errant wisp just swim beneath the pale eyelashes, slide through a mournful eye and emerge, eel-like from his ear? For a moment I had the strangest fancy that the pipe was smoking him, recycling his ectoplasm -- that physical manifestation of spirit.

"Stop it at once!" I cried with a voice far more assertive than I ever managed when he was alive. My mind raced, guilt mixed with fear.

Perhaps I shouldn't have done it. His antique steam-launch had been his joy every Sunday -- its copper boiler and shrill whistle. "There goes the Commodore" people would say as he puffed up and down the rush-rimmed lake, the golden braid on his cap gleaming in the sunshine, his telescope clamped to his eye.

I would not be reprimanded by the deceased. A father with only one lung and tumours the size of sausages had no need of boats and fenders, or winches and anchors, or need to hear the shushing waves beneath his bow. Bills had mounted for 24-hour care, oxygen tanks, and tweed-clad nurses to push him about, querulous in his bath-chair. I had to choose -- become the head of the family. I sold his boat.

The head stopped dead, then swivelled like a battle cruiser's gun-turret until the pipe pointed straight at me. Deep within his pupils some dark tadpoles of matter twisted and spun. Smoke coiled at the pipe rim, and then swarmed about his thin lips and nostrils. The head undulated alarmingly, like a bulging sail spilling in the teeth of a gale.

"Mutiny!" he barked. The crumpled head shot out the window, a grey empty fuzz-ball, arcing over the muffled park, a shadow on the sombre lake, falling at last into far-off shrubbery, to bounce then puff into disgruntled nothingness.

**

ART
Title: Father Frost and the step-daughter, Artist: Ivan Bilibin, Style: Art Nouveau (Modern), Genre: illustration

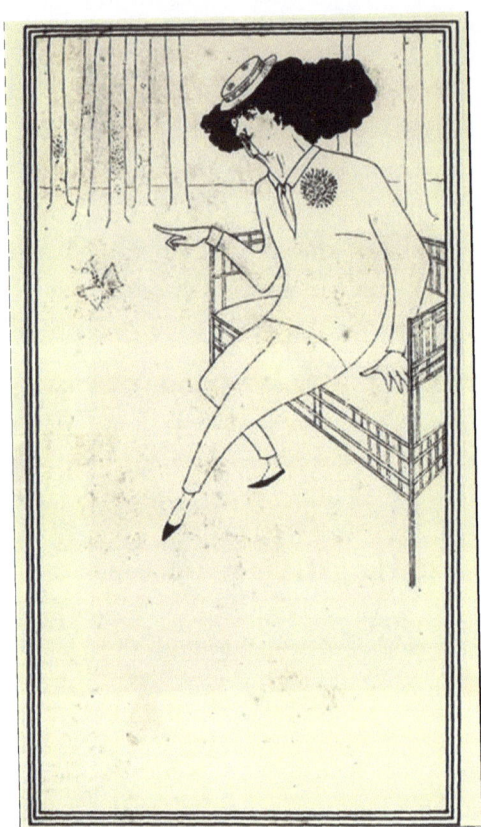

Whistle like a Clanger

By Bill West

She sleeps, head cradled in your arm. Her head, like a moon, low in the night sky. You want to blast off, land in some deep crater, and explore her secrets. Her ear invites you. It makes you think of a pale sea-shell crater. Uninvited you slide helter-skelter, down into the darkness.

Wax walls ripple, they twist into shapes; white rocking-chairs, tables and dolls houses. You drop past figures that sprout like mushrooms which come alive. Morph rides past on a nailbrush, Clangers whistle to you, waving their four-fingered wave.
(Come on now, whistle like a Clanger!)

And then you land and bounce for a while, slowly up and down on her red, velvet eardrum.

At the centre is a puckered hole. You slide through; head first, like being born.

You emerge from the cradle of a giant water-lily and look out over a dimpled pool. Frogs with bulging eyes menace, snapping dragonflies with whiplash tongues. You dance from leaf to leaf, leviathan goldfish below circle, waiting for you to fall.

You scramble ashore and push past giant grasses and prickled nettle stems, until you reach a clearing.

The giant green caterpillar sits on a toadstool, with his fez and hookah pipe. He has curly silk slippers on each of his sixteen feet. They wiggle like red buttons as he sucks on his pipe. He blows out rainbow clouds that swirl like mist, stream like swallows that swerve and twitter as they fly away. "She's watching!" he mumbles before turning away.

And you are floating in darkness, stars twinkle above and below. The stars swell, drawing near, silver at first but turning to gold as they grow, each one an eye with heavy lids and veils of eyelashes. They watch.

You want to hide but as you twist and turn each eye fills with a milky-way of tears. They wash you like warm milk. You tumble and turn, down twisting ducts until you are squeezed like a pearl from her breast.

You wake with your head on her belly. Your head moves up and down with each breath. You whistle like a Clanger.
(Come on now, whistle like a Clanger.)

***

ART
Title, Caricature of James McNeill Whistler, Artist, Aubrey Beardsley, Style: Art Nouveau (Modern), Genre: caricature, Location: National Gallery of Art, Washington, DC, US

PART TWO

Every Preposterous Thing

"Alice laughed. 'There's no use trying,' she said. 'One can't believe impossible things.'

"I daresay you haven't had much practice," said the Queen. "When I was your age, I always did it for half-an-hour a day. Why, sometimes I've believed as many as six impossible things before breakfast ..." Lewis Carroll

Swans on Boderg, Mari Fitzpatrick, Acrylic on Card

PAINTED PICTURES

… there are only three primary colours and they change depending on their given work space. BUT THEN THERE'S *regular workspace AND there's Burton workspace. A space that can shout and soothe without ever speaking. His keys and 'tweens illustrate everyman skies.*

Take your mind back: It's 2010 and it's Alice time again, This time it's Tim Burtons' mark that's been placed on the soul of the project. For if any character has soul it's Alice, little did Dodgson realise what he was igniting when he put pen to paper in 1862 to transcribe the children's story that he had composed to entertain his friend's daughters one summer's afternoon while rowing on the Isis in Oxford. Alice Liddell was 10 year's old at the time and the youngest of the three sisters, and it would take another three years of her pestering him before he agreed to self-publish and to have the story printed under his pen name.

Now it is Burton turn to share his rhyme, rhythm and vision as he spells or even spills the child's tale through a contemporary coloured spectrum. Trained by Disney in the 80s, he's back in the fold for this production. And for this one Alice gets to grow up and dance to a colourists' tune.

The Alice story opens-out on a homely scene that is depicted in soft, warm, tones in an country house setting; from the look of the fashion and staging one gets a feel for an olden time.

There's a Stoker and Shelly flavour trapped in the introduction that has a rich tapestry laid down, which is one of mystery and intrigue as we listen in as a man discusses work and travel plans with his associates. The flavour of the conversation is good natured; this viewer's curiosity was stroked, I wanted to find out more about the people who lived in this old-style manor house, and who wore the old-style clothes.

Burton's reputation preceded the show, he is such a well-known character in his own right: the man who gave the world such a classic original with his production of "Edward Scissorhands," and the man who stroked and stoked Washington Irvings' "Sleepy Hollow" with grey and blue filters was now taken a shot at an old favourite: A children's favourite. But the viewer has not long to wait on story development as the plot-line was cast in the first few minutes when Alice appeared at the drawing room door, sleepy-eyed and anxious, just woken from a nightmare; she comes looking for comfort and her dad takes her back to bed and soothes her sighs as he enquires about her wonderland dream of blue caterpillars and smiling cats and the scene fades through filtered hues of green and blue, and shaded golden yellows shadows and we're there in story time --in a Burton's 2K drama.

Adventures in Wonderland was first printed, in Oxford, in 1865, Carroll had 50 copies printed for friends, it had a limited run and was pulled to correct copy when John Tinnell complained about the print quality of his illustrations. A second edition was ordered from printers in London, and it was put out to market in 1866, and Alice's Adventures in Wonderland entered the public imagination

We are fast forwarded 10 years to meet a 20 year old Alice and her mum riding in a carriage on their way to a garden party. It's a lovely countryside image with forestry edging the road; swans winging their way through a bright, blue sky; it's a spring/summer day, a day saturated in primary colour and clear light. When they arrive at the house, they are greeted by their hosts who are long time family friends, and we are given a foreshadow of the wonderland characters as we meet-up with some of the guests--having already met the cat and caterpillar in the first scene--we're now introduced to the *Tweddle Dum/Dee* twin sisters, and we get a chance to focus into Burton's vision of their real-world-rooted-personality as he uses them as a bridge to introduce the current local gossip; the idea of an Alice engagement to Hamish, a maiden aunt who they claim has lost her looks: Alice's sister and her fiancée who we're told has an eye for the ladies,-- and of course we meet Hamish, with his colourful mad-hatter hair,--he is the Lord in Waiting: In waiting for Alice to accept his marriage proposal and in this scene as he waits to get down on one knee to propose in front of the party, an idea that was prompted by the *Tweedle Dum/Dee* sisters takes hold in the young woman's imagination and she runs, and once again follows the *White Rabbit* through the magical door and once more trips into *Wonderland.*

Up to her trip down the rabbit hole, the garden party tone is layered in suggestive dialogue, in fashionable dress, in party chat and family chatter. There's little real colour shading, other than regular story and its usual measured dimension that one might find in any fine production, like background story fillers, key points and staging, but then isn't it in real-life that we meet exaggeration like the *Tweedle Dum/Dee* sisters, for what else have we to work with? Writers, artists, cartoonists all exaggerate our similarities and differences for effect, or at least the good ones do.

So, Alice runs. Follows the Rabbit. And falls back into her Wonderland dream. Over five minutes of shades and tones, like those in the intro scene, tones bringing the viewer's mind back to the first scene only to bring it forward again and slowly ease the eye through from 12. 43 minutes in, when Alice looks down the hole and trips and falls through the umbers and golds that are littered with images of books and music : she springs off a bed, crashes through a ceiling , continues to fall until she eventually lands right side up and proceeds to grow, and shrink and find the key to the door to wonderland we're now up at 18.09 minutes with little or no dialogue, just atmospheric strokes. Really!

It should feel like forever when one considers that one A4 page is required to make up one minute of screen dialogue. Six minutes is a long time to keep the viewer's attention. to ask them to watch a head- over-heels trip—a silent tumble. Yet this 6 minutes of silent colour screening, talked, chatted and screamed to connect us once again to an Alice storyscape, But then colour connects us all at our core as it creates atmospheres that we step into in our day-to-day life, it can be one of peace, beauty, fear, or terror and all the in-between tones of intrigue that make up our individual stories. For one's attention affects one'sperception.

Artists like Burton, the good ones, have always used colour to share their vision and to storm worlds. For they illustrate life for all of us, as they pin our eye on carefully selected targets, on the screen, or on a canvas, they know that even as we all live similar lives and together step through the seasons, we own our subjective vision and our own black and white suggestions comes in tones and shades that starkly illustrate the beauty or dread that's found in any day.

For seeing and understanding are connected!

We say I see when we agree with another, we say I see when we figure we know something to be true. We see to know, and we create ICONS of the best of the work whether we find it on screen or canvas, work like Edvard Munch's "Scream" which sold for over a hundred million Euros in the mid noughties

… Munch is quoted as saying that: "Nature is not only all that is visible to the eye... it also includes the inner pictures of the soul." Edvard Munch

Alice, as a young adult arrives back into her dreamland,and backgrounds are laid down as we once again see her meet-up with the smiling cat, the blue caterpillar and our amazing mad hatter, as dreamy sepia lifts-up stark blue,and red and purple flowers that float freely from her and our wonderland friends as we get to hear and see the new stories in the ongoing drama of the *Jabberwocky,* the *Red Queen* and her sister the *White Queen* and we watch and wait for resolutions for Alice finally remembers her promise and accepts why she's back in place.

T. Hee : ""the application of colour is equally as important as the drawing itself" and everyone has a colour that is determined by individual personality and character." (Johnson and Thomas, The Illusion of Life, P 268, Rev. Ed, ISBN: 0-7868-6070-7)

Winter and spring tones illustrate the personalities that drive the story line. Red for anger and danger. The *Red Queen* will own her day, her courtiers will live the fearful life tht she has designed as she takes -off the heads of those who displease her and ruins her fun, there is no warmth to be had in her landscape, for by her very actions and anticipations she strokes fear into hearts as she threatens all who get in her way. Her tone seeps from her personal boundaries and colours all in her presence. It is dark yet bright with anger and fear as contrasts are toned and colour washed and placed in scenes to bolster the emotion.

But Spring, (our *Queen of Hearts*) who lives to be governed by the *Red Queen* is still dressed in blossom and lily tones, in soft pinks and peach, as she awaits a saviour, for it is written in the book, depicted on the scroll of life, that Alice will step back in to save the day. And together, she and the *White Queen* will stand back-to-back as the storm clouds gather over a desolate grey field that is mirrored in pregnant tones of black and white. In a chessboard collection of clouds.

It's the dead of winter as the battle begins, and the royal champions step-up to the plate. Alice carries the sword of the *White Queen,* the *Jabberwocky* carries the energy of her sister the *Red Queen*. The *White Rabbit* plays the battle trumpet and *Alice,* like *David* in the bible story, enters the arena stage left, to face down a battle ready army led out in the field by the *Red Queen*. An army spread out and standing shoulder-to-shoulder in a huge show of force, and just when one expects them to attack they open ranks to make way for the *Jabberwocky* and we see the monster break out of a cocoon, lift out of the earth and as their armed combat commences, we get to see who gets to do the impossible: who gets to do 6 impossible things before breakfast and who wins.

It's victory for the *White Queen*, it's victory for *Alice*, It's victory for *The Mad Hatter* who dances the Futterwack, and as Alice drinks the blood of the *Jabberwocky* gifted from the *White Queen* she pops back into the engagement scene in the garden party. It's not the end, though it's near it, but I'm not spoiling that here for those who haven't seen it.

It's victory for Tim Burton too, as his vision of the story makes way for more. Will we see *Alice* and the *Hatter* again? Will they become an item? There's a one! but who knows, for there are only three primary colours and they change depending on their given workspace. And then there is regular workspace and there's Burtons' workspace. A space that can shout and soothe without ever speaking. His keys and 'tweens illustrate everyman stories.

In our world we are surrounded by beauty on a day-to-day basis: sunrises, sunsets, misty mornings that shimmers light on lakes and rivers and we become immune, as we race from work, to home, to schools, busy with regular living. And then an artist or film maker comes along and repositions our focus.

Carroll did that when he wrote *Alice's Adventures in Wonderland,* Disney did similar when he made *Snow White and The Seven Dwarfs* back in the day. and Burton did it with this 2010 production of *Alice in Wonderland.*

Fin
Mari Fitzpatrick 2020,
Mari Fitzpatrick is the managing editor of "The Linnet's Wings."

THE SECRET MARRIAGE

by

Susan Tepper

Portrait of a Lady
(unfinished)
Gustav Klimt
Date: 1917 - 1918
Style: Symbolism
Period: Late works
Genre: portrait
Media: pen, ink, watercolor, paper

Ritual

"She left? You mean left left?"

"Apparently."

Sweating profusely, Mickey is leaning under the striped awning chugging a juice. "Apparently?"

"They need to beef up the amenities in this club." I wipe my face with a napkin. "Why not an indoor juice bar, too? With chairs. And tables. We pay enough to belong..."

He waves me off. "Ah...you're a bad loser."

He beat my ass in squash. Again. We do it anyway. It's a ritual.

"Apparently?" Mickey says again. "Your wife bucks and that's all you got?"

"Should I cry?"

I mean, isn't that pretty dramatic?"

"Paula is the dramatic gesture."

"What's that s'posed to mean?"

"It's who she is is all I'm saying."

Giving me one of his low-lidded stares, he takes off his glasses, wrings out his sweat band.

"Mickey?"

"Yeah?"

"You have to be back at the hospital?" I swig the last of my juice and chuck the bottle in a recycle bin.

"Eventually. You?"

"I have coverage."

"OK," he says. "BINGS. But I gotta shower first."

BINGS being one of those places my old man used to call joints. Right off the Northern Parkway. Ours the only cars in the lot – its filled with contractor vans, SUV's, pick-ups parked sloppy. Younger guys hit BINGS for pool, the betting, the stacked waitresses said to be HOOTERS rejects.

Walking in ahead of me, Mickey calls out to Sid who grins and tosses him a beer across the bar. Another ritual. He's moving fast, straight toward a booth directly under the cold air vent. I'm about to say bad idea – what with the lousy ventilation and all, probably standing water, legionella spores. But Mickey's already settled in.

"Uh... Mickey?"

"What?"

"Forget it." Heaving myself in the booth I plant my elbows on a thick, wood slab of a table. Dark varnish carved with hearts, phone numbers, messages to score dope, sex, whatever is for sale – people can't resist when there's wood and a steak blade at the ready. BINGS, as usual, jammed with the mid-day crowd. A big group around the pool table. Some skinny Goldilocks on speed screeching after each shot.

"Chicago! Now there's a game with balls!" she yells.

"Shut up!" I yell back. She looks up surprised, her red mouth forming an O.

Mickey burps. "Take it easy, pal."

Years ago I put a pool table in our basement. Full sized, antique, solid mahogany lip with deeply embossed pockets made out of Spanish saddle leather. A real beauty. Paula would never play. Below ground level depresses me was the excuse.

The random clacking of balls; like atoms splitting if you could hear that. Try explaining to Paula. Thirty years living with random violence – the ER is a car wreck a minute if you stop to assess. There can be some comfort in the counting of things. Sure, it gives a false sense of control. But all the same. The practice of Medicine. Capable of twisting your brain into snakes. The pretentious docs like calling it art. You could puke.

"So, Paula." Mickey's looking around.

Don't expect her to come walking in, I'm thinking.

He's scratching his chin, on a jag now. "It's got to be one of her old jaunts. Paula gets bored at home, goes back to her old tour guide run around the world gig." He snort-laughs blowing into the neck of his beer bottle. "Southeast Asia? Madagascar? Where will she end up now you suppose?"

"How the hell should I know?" I laugh, too; not really; rubbing the back of my neck slow like you rub the neck of a dog. It feels good – the rubbing. I signal the girl at the bar to come over. "She fucking... last week. No note, nothing."

The waitress struts over in that swig-swag way, lots of leg, short checkered apron, a square dance kind of white top gathered low to show cleavage when she bends.

"Scotch, double, neat," I tell her.

She turns to Mickey. "Another beer?"

Staring at the girl he shakes his head stupidly.

You cardiac guys are supposed to stay pumped, I'm thinking. No falling in love for half an hour, not in this dump, anyway. When she walks away I tell him, "Don't even think about it."

"What?"

She comes right back, does the dip from the waist when she puts down my drink. Touché. She winks then moves along.

"Listen, Mickey." His eyes are following the waitress. "Mickey." I rap on the table with my knuckles. "Keep this Paula thing to yourself, OK? I don't want it getting around the hospital."

He puts out a hand which I choose to ignore.

"Steady. Steady pardner. Paula does this sort of thing. She'll get bored and come running home. You'll see. Mark my words." He's talking way too much. He's already mapped out the deal.

I down the scotch in one long swallow. "Isn't that beside the point?"

The wedding party
Henri Rousseau
Original Title: La noce
Date: c.1905
Style: Naïve Art (Primitivism)
Genre: portrait
Media: oil, canvas
Location: Musée de l'Orangerie, Paris, France

DWINDLING: THE SHRINKING CITIZEN

by Stephen Zelnick

John Milton never attended a political convention, but *Paradise Lost* depicts satanic demagogy and citizens dwindled to mere onlookers, overwhelmed by giant voices. In the great hall of Pandemonium, the rebels against God gather to decide next steps. Giant angels, now tarnished by betrayal, swarm into the vast auditorium. They are too large to fit; so, Satan downsizes them. The rebellion's central committee retain their vast dimensions and thundering voices. Milton, alert to the political crisis of his time -- feudal authority fractured and politics now opened to th bold and aggressive – warns his readers against brilliant and unscrupulous leaders able to bend the great many to their will:

Behold a wonder! They but now who seemed
In bigness to surpass Earth's giant sons,
Now less than smallest dwarfs, in narrow room
Throng numberless

Thus incorporeal Spirits to smallest forms
Reduced their shapes immense, and were at large,
Though without number still, amidst the hall
Of that infernal court. But far within,
And in their own dimensions like themselves,
The great Seraphic Lords and Cherubim
In close recess and secret conclave sat,

High on a throne of royal state, which far
Outshone the wealth of Ormus and of Ind,
Or where the gorgeous East with richest hand
Showers on her kings barbaric pearl and gold,
Satan exalted sat, ...

The rebelling angels imagine themselves consulted in this conclave of the great, deceived by Pandemonium's grandiose architecture and the resounding rhetoric. The decisions have been fixed by "the great seraphic Lords and Cherubim, / in close recess and secret conclave." This mockery of democracy (demockracy) inspires the rebel warriors to cling to their masters. Blind to their subservience, they imagine their fate is their choice. The great hall emboldens them to imagine truth is determined by their numbers and the grandeur of their leaders. And all this, long before the massive screens and thundering sound systems of our own day.

[pic]

[Pandemonium overwhelms the imagination even of former angels familiar with heavenly wonders. Grand architecture recruits them for grand deeds even as it enforces their insignificance.]

41

Milton has spotted the willingness of the great many to be welcomed to governing and then fooled about their role in it. Swift warns us in his own delightfully savage way, and the actions of the Founders of the United States in the 1780s demonstrate a real-world instance of an elite misleading the great many to a false democracy. Melville's Moby-Dick dives deep into the same theme, as do Chayevsky's "Network" and the recent film "Downsizing". The crisis of democracy is nothing new, as Thucydides and Plato illuminated, in Athens at the beginning.

1

In Swift's *Gulliver's Travels* (1726) Gulliver awakens a captive of Lilliputians, bound by a thousand threads and encircled by an army of minuscule but bold warriors. Gulliver is bewildered, but gentle and receptive to his captivity. Although powerful enough to trample their courts and cities, he falls under the spell of regal authority and the law which binds him by imagination more firmly than by packing thread. The Great Many, can agree to accept the most preposterous explanation and symbolic assertion of the hostile powers that bind them – Gulliver, one of us, is gullible.

[pic]

[Gulliver is bewildered by his diminutive captors but willing to cede his power to ceremonies of state. Gulliver is kind and cooperative, and a perfect victim for the machinations of a tyrannical government.]

Awakening, Gulliver is addressed by the emperor's emissary. Though Gulliver understands none of his speech, he is impressed by his comportment. "He acted every part of an orator, and I could observe many periods of threatenings, and others of promises, pity, and kindness. I answered in a few words, but in the most submissive manner, ..." Gulliver falls into the proportional delusion, attributing grand motives to this miniscule official. Gulliver observes he could easily "seize forty or fifty of the first that came in my reach and dash them against the ground." However, Gulliver resists this impulse, overwhelmed by the arts of political grandeur to accept these tiny beings at their own measure.

When he arrives, the emperor is impressive: "His excellency, having mounted on the small of my right leg, advanced forwards up to my face, with about a dozen of his retinue; and producing his credentials under the signet royal, which he applied close to my eyes, spoke about ten minutes without any signs of anger, but with a kind of determinate resolution,..." The royal signet is impressive as is the emperor's manner, but it is his physical presence that awes Gulliver: "He is taller by almost the breadth of my nail, than any of his court; which alone is enough to strike an awe into the beholders. His features are strong and masculine, with an Austrian lip and arched nose, his complexion olive, his countenance erect, his body and limbs well proportioned, all his motions graceful, and his deportment

majestic." Swift invites us to enjoy his comparison with the Hapsburg facial deformity, a recognized signet of its own throughout Europe. But Gulliver immediately adapts his diminishment and dwindling subjectivity.

[pic]

[A giant, Gulliver bends the knee to his miniscule masters. He is proud to serve them in war and to receive their commendations. Once he has served them, the state must destroy him to protect itself.]

v

Once assured his giant visitor has accepted the Lilliputian measure of things, the prince has Gulliver pledge his fealty: "I made my acknowledgements by prostrating myself at his majesty's feet: but he commanded me to rise; and after many gracious expressions, which, to avoid the censure of vanity, I shall not repeat, he added, 'that he hoped I should prove a useful servant, and well deserve all the favors he had already conferred upon me, or might do for the future.'" Gulliver as yet knows nothing of his prince's treacheries, but ceremony and trappings of feudal eminence are sufficient to exact his pledge of service. He is like the rest of us, entangled in the web of ceremony and convention to surrender his freedom and good sense. As the emperor's cruelty becomes clear, Gulliver struggles to free his mind. State honors – for dousing the blaze in the empress' chambers -- enhance his delusions. His submergence into the Lilliputian madness is complete when he captures the enemy fleet and earns the title of "nardac" ... "the highest title of honor among them" as he boasts.

Nonetheless, Gulliver's service to the state causes him nothing but trouble. The empress rages at his discourteous method of dowsing the fire, and the admiralty is furious at Gulliver's easy victory over the rival fleet. They plot against him and convince the emperor to agree to put out Gulliver's eyes, reducing his danger to Lilliput, while preserving his size and strength for public works and war. Once his usefulness ends, he can be starved to death. A courier delivers the emperor's sentence in the official and authoritative form: "That if his majesty, in consideration of your services, and pursuant to his own merciful disposition, would please to spare your life, and only give orders to put out both your eyes, he humbly conceived, that by this expedient justice might in some measure be satisfied, and all the world would applaud the lenity of the emperor, as well as the fair and generous proceedings of those who have the honor to be his counsellors."

One would expect Gulliver to rebel. However, as the emissary explains:

"That the loss of your eyes would be no impediment to your bodily strength, by which you might still be useful to his majesty; that blindness is an addition to courage, by concealing dangers from us; that the fear you had for your eyes, was the greatest difficulty in bringing over the enemy's fleet, and it would be sufficient for you to see by the eyes of the ministers, since the greatest princes do no more."

Gulliver, an exemplary citizen, accepts this judgment as normal and just. He remarks: "if I had then known the nature of princes and ministers, which I have since observed in many other courts, and their methods of treating criminals less obnoxious than myself, I should, with great alacrity and readiness, have submitted to so easy a punishment. But hurried on by the precipitancy of youth," Gulliver escapes by fleeing the emperor's domain, yet taking with him feelings of carrying with him the burden of guilt.

Swift's satire targets the cruelty of kings, the misuse of science, insignificant differences that divide nations internally and from one another, and so on; but at the heart of Swift's satire is Gulliver, a good man who means well but is bound by invisible threads of imagination that keep him and the rest of us enslaved to systems that mean us harm. He suffers from the dwindling of imagination, a disease that makes him small, helpless, and insignificant. Though he is a giant, stepping over towering buildings in Lilliput and wading their seas, he is trapped in a net of illusion; in a moment of clarity, the honest citizen remarks "I really began to imagine myself dwindled many degrees below my usual size."

2

[pic]

[The U.S. Constitution was designed to invite government by the people and also forcefully restrict it. The Constitution protected property rights and the interests of large landowners and merchants.]

In the United States, we now have diminished expectations for democracy. Alexis de Tocqueville in the 1830s marveled at how well-informed and energetic in political debate Americans were. Through the next century, waves of immigrants arrived, many seeking a nation "of, by and for the people." Democracy at most requires a state ruled by the people, or as a republic at least friendly to the people's liberty and dignity. But 18th century Founders doubted the people's trustworthiness and recorded their misgivings. The Constitution excluded women, transients, and the poor from the exercise of citizenship. One could argue those people lacked experience and a sufficient stake in outcomes to promise reliable judgment. People merely passing through or owning no property might make decisions without suffering the consequences. Women and enslaved people had limited experience directing their own lives let alone governing others. Some of these direct exclusions persisted for two centuries, and some remain.

Political philosophers have long challenged the competence of "the people", considering them ignorant, formed for slavish lives, and needing others to lead them. Some considered the demos limited by nature to pursuing animal pleasures. When, for example, Moses went off to confer with God, the Israelites erected a Golden Calf and fell to worshipping lust. In Plato's Republic the demos embrace novelty and disorderly delights at the cost of sanity and justice. Machiavelli's Florentines, two millennia on, are credulous and easily misled.

[pic]

[The House of Representatives struggles to reflect the people's will. Originally, each Congressperson represented no more than 30,000 persons; now the number is 750,000.]

While the Founders welcomed the great many to participate in government, they established strict limits. The House of Representatives (the "people's house") was a gathering of representatives only. Direct democracy may have functioned locally, but distance and slow travel made large gatherings impractical, and cities later produced greater numbers and collisions of cultures. Today Congress members represent 750,000 people, guaranteeing they will respond only to their wealthiest and most prominent constituents. The rich merchants and powerful landowners who shaped the republic expected the "People's House" to be raucous and subject to demagogy; and so, provided a Senate of wise, experienced men to restrain them. Like the Senate, the President was chosen not by popular vote but by an electoral college. States were accorded two Senators, no matter their population, corrupting the force of the popular vote. Amending the Constitution was made nearly impossible. The Founders' republic respected property but not the people. Recently, Leona Helmsley, a person of great wealth, explained, "We don't pay taxes. Only the little people pay taxes."

[pic]

[Sheldon Wolin's Democracy, Inc. (2008) is a brave account of the descent of our democratically-inclined republic into "managed democracy".]

The crisis of democracy in our time comes from the concentration of wealth and the nation's expansion into empire, with needs and interests too weighty to be left to the people. We have arrived at "managed democracy", the illusion of free choice, controlled by economic interests with sharply focused tools to compel consent. Mass culture of the 20th C., especially in war time, produced powerful weapons of coercion to organize the imagination and will of nations. The same processes that advertise deodorant, automobiles, cheap eateries, and soft drinks now herd citizens into safe pens of agreeableness and narrow chutes of destruction. The dwindling of the citizen, his helplessness and anxiety, is now the project of the imperial state commanded by powerful corporations, exceeding the wealth and power of nations, led by ruthless commanders of reality, operating beyond law and moral restraint or tradition. Corporate states reduce citizens to spectators in a drama of large gestures and grand rhetoric, in the imaginary halls of modern media. None of this works without the agreeableness of the gullible, pledged to be orderly and convenient to their masters, who would pluck out their eyes if need be.

3

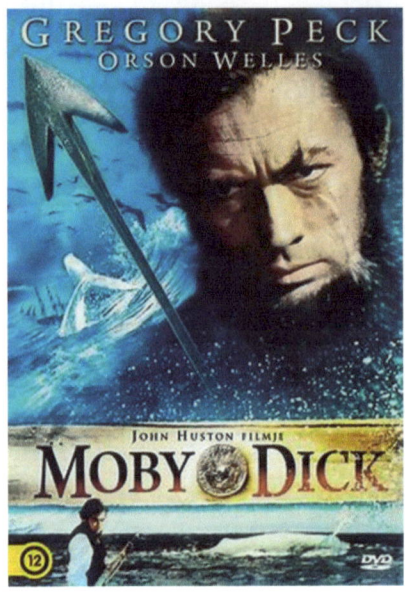

[pic]

[Herman Melville's Moby-Dick (1851) explores the dangers of illusory democracy easily corrupted by a demagogue of genius working upon the dis-ease of the people.]

Moby-Dick explores this theme of dwindling democracy, casting Captain Ahab as Satan and the Pequod's crew as giant personalities diminished by the force of a master demagogue. Melville dramatizes the worries that haunted the Founders and that even de Tocqueville acknowledged. Ahab is surprised at the ease with which he enlists his crew in his demonic project: "'Twas not so hard a task. I thought to find one stubborn, at the least; but my one cogged circle fits into all their various wheels, and they revolve. Or, if you will, like so many ant-hills of powder, they all stand before me; and I their match. Oh, hard! that to fire others, the match itself must needs be wasting! What I've dared, I've willed; and what I've willed, I'll do!" (Chapter 37).

The Pequod's crew draws its peculiar genius from the hard-working masses of all the world, indigenous peoples from cultures East and West, and talents of every kind required in the whaling trade. The ship is an elegant hierarchy, from the cabin boys, to the master carpenter and skinners, to the majestic harpooners, and the managers (Stubb, Flask, and Starbuck), and mad Ahab overseeing it all. The crew, like the people of the United States, come from everywhere and lose the cultures they have fled. They are forged into a new identity – rootless and yearning for great adventures and titanic accomplishments. Unquiet souls, they are ready-made for Ahab's exploitation, molding their restlessness to the bitter shape of his vengeance. The Founders feared majoritarian tyranny and obstructed democratic power (only the House of Representatives was elected directly). Melville envisions the threat to the republic issuing from the political talents of a great leader grasping power over a demos unanchored by traditions, social habits, and settled institutions.

[pic]

[The Pequod gathers heroes from many lands, races, and cultures welded into a community chasing its own destruction.]

The traditional account of democratic corruption identifies flattery as the source, and Ahab caters to their self-esteem, praises their hardihood and exalts their ambition.[i] Ahab, however, achieves his pre-eminence by understanding the psychological needs of his men. Ahab knows that his countrymen are restless, divided between the rigors of a hard, laboring life, and the dreams of vast endeavors in a boundless landscape. The inquietude of soul that drives Ishmael to sea is a national disease, waiting for a canny leader to exploit it. Even Ishmael, our Gulliver, clever and irreverent as he is, is not immune:

"I, Ishmael, was one of that crew; my shouts had gone up with the rest; my oath had been welded with theirs; and stronger I shouted, and more did I hammer and clinch my oath, because of the dread in my soul. A wild mystical, sympathetical feeling was in me; Ahab's quenchless feud seemed mine. With greedy ears I learned the history of that murderous monster against whom I and all others had taken our oaths of violence and revenge."

Ahab has the power of his madness: "There is one God that is Lord over the earth, and one Captain that is lord over the Pequod" (Chapter 109), but he is also a master Con-man, a genius at dramaturgy. Ahab constructs three bewitching moments of political theater: (1) the doubloon -- and its exotic heraldry of mountain, eagle and sun -- focusses his crew's imagination (Ch. 36 and Ch. 99); (2) Ahab's mastering of St. Elmo's fire – here appearing to command nature itself (Ch. 119); and, finally, with a mountebank's skill, Ahab re-magnetizes a needle compass, astonishing his crew (Ch. 124). Ahab fashions himself as a force challenging both God and the Devil to redeem mankind from subservience to the galling indignities of life.[ii]

[pic]

[Captain Ahab, ruling like a God over his little world at sea, is a master at manipulating the fears and dreams of his crew.]

Ishmael as narrator demonstrates his philosophical agility and endless skepticism. Yet, Ishmael cannot resist Ahab's call to rebellion against all decency and order. Starbuck, a wiser man, with home and hearth to protect and the reality of commercial responsibilities gnawing at him, also, in the final instance, is drowned in the maelstrom of Ahab's imperial arrogance. They and the titans of craft and power, the immense harpooners, fit the cogs of Ahab's great wheel, and shrink into the machinery, having surrendered their minds and souls to Ahab.

4

[pic]

In "Downsizing" (2017) citizens accept their physical diminishment in a culture that has already shrunk their power and sense of self.]

The Sci-Fi film "Downsizing" (2017) was an ambitious project that several A-list actors rejected. "Downsizing" was not a commercial or a critical success, and critics viewed the film as an entertainment rather than a meditation on today's world. Treating science fiction lightly is a common mistake, as if a tradition that includes "Metropolis", "The Day the Earth Stood Still", "The Body-Snatchers", "Twilight Zone", "Soylent Green", and "Blade-Runner" has not been whispering to us all along about what we have become and what fate awaits us.

"Downsizing" explores dwindling in three settings – Norway, the US, and the Third World. Norwegian scientists, fearing overpopulation, devise a way to shrink human beings from 1.8 meters (6 feet) to 12.9 centimeters (about 5 inches). As the lead scientist, now downsized, explains to a startled audience, the human footprint imposed on nature can be reduced, with no degradation of life experience once the downsized settle into communities of the super-small. To demonstrate, a full-size assistant carries onstage a single trash bag, partially full, representing the output of a downsized community over four months' time. A happy community of the downsized, young and old and of every ethnicity, waves to the audience from a metal cart as the audience greets its future prospects in a new balance of nature.

[pic]

[Science has found a way to shrink human beings to Lilliputian dimensions – in Norway to relieve pressure on a stressed environment. U. S. citizens adopt this outrage to nature to pay their bills.]

We shift then ten years into the future and into the life of Paul Safranek (Matt Damon), a normal American -- congenial, weighted down by financial worries, tolerating a job below his aspirations, hungering after pleasures dangling just out of reach, but accepting it all as his dose of life. Safranek is pudgy and not particularly attractive, pleasant but his affect suppressed; everyone mispronounces his name, his identity barely acknowledged. His wife wants more out of life -- a bigger kitchen and ultra-modern shower -- a house to keep pace with the Jones'. With downsizing, their savings of $158,000 would be worth $12.5M, where even the grandest mansion is a doll house, and living costs are dramatically reduced. Unlike the Norwegians, the downsizing incentive in the US is purely economic – Audrey can have her dream house and Paul a way to escape his pinched existence.

[pic]

[Downsized persons can fulfill their dreams in a doll-house mansion in Leisureland.]

5

The detailed process of downsizing is painstaking and funny. With all body hair removed and teeth replaced, subjects awaken to the shock of their diminishment. The newly tiny are lifted from their beds on spatulas, and in recovery the nurse delivers an immense saltine. The downsized now are mice; their doll house world, Leisureland, recalls "The Prisoner" and "Pleasantville", a cheerful world of the well-to-do with nothing to do. He lives at "Navajo Orchards", a subdivision with the curving roadways and cul-de-sacs of our soul-less suburbs. But his wife, repelled by the cosmetic aggressions, refuses downsizing; Paul's divorce bankrupts him, leaving him living in a modest condo and a job, fielding phone complaints for Land's End clothing. As in Gulliver's Travels nature's violation appears normal; in the US, as economic rationality and an appeal to the latest thing. Safranek cannot change his circumstances, where the bank's loan officer determines the limit of his hopes. He lives in a managed democracy, where citizenship has no meaning.

The satiric force, in Swift, is how citizens accept bizarre conditions as normal. Gulliver will accept having his eyes put out, because it is a regular process of state, duly recognized by the court. His doom is pronounced with official ceremony, and with legal language and paperwork. Paul Safranek – like Gulliver, pleasant and agreeable and willing always to cooperate – is persuaded by brochures and showrooms and model houses and sales pitches that dwindling is sensible. We become our bank balances, victims of hunger and debt that can never be satisfied. In "Downsizing" the state has disappeared, replaced by the corporation, upon which the citizen can exert no weight. Paul is helpless and but some sort of happy, as his wan smile testifies.

[pic]

[Paul Safranek talks it through with a tiny salesman of downsizing.]

6

In Paradise Lost and Gulliver's Travels state power creates a dwindled normalcy. In "Downsizing" state power, for the American, recedes behind the force of consumption and advertising. Unlike Norwegians, Americans are oblivious to the threat of an exhausted planet and pursue their lives getting and spending and competing with neighbors. "Downsizing" is much like "Network", where in a key scene the mega-industrialist (Arthur Jensen) reveals to the addled news reader that corporate power rules his world. "Downsizing" depicts neo-liberalism, where no tensions appear in the smooth progress from cradle to grave now made rational by corporate management. Paddy Chayefsky's "Network", a harder-edged satire, names names.

"I'm as mad as hell, and I'm not gonna take this anymore!"

[pic]

[Anchorman Howard Beale (Peter Finch) snaps in rage and despair and threatens to bring the nation with him in "Network" (1976).]

The film "Network" (1976), script by Paddy Chayefsky, has become famous for its iconic bellow "I'm mad as hell, and I'm not gonna take it anymore", by the unhinged TV news anchor Howard Beale. Beale has lost his mind reporting endless war, a crime infested NYC, and boundless corruption; but his listeners echo his cry, lifting their windows in the night to cry out in despair. Chayefsky's satire targets TV, loveless love, revolution as business. However, at a critical moment, he lifts the veil of illusions to reveal the global network of corporations that direct human destiny and mock all previous understandings of nations and ideologies, and, indeed, of God Himself.

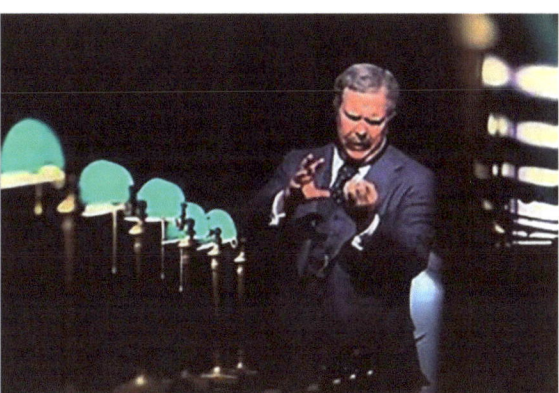

[pic]

[If the man behind the curtain explained himself, he would be Arthur Jensen (New Beatty), the ultimate salesman, charged with reining in the madness of Beale and its threat to world corporatism.]

In an antique corporate boardroom, Jensen has this to say:

You have meddled with the primal forces of nature, Mr. Beale, and I won't have it.... You are an old man who thinks of nations and peoples. There are no nations. There are no peoples. There are no Russians. There are no Arabs. There are no Third Worlds. There is no West.

There is only one holistic system of systems. One vast and interwoven, interacting, multivariate, multinational dominion of dollars. Petrol dollars, electro dollars, multi dollars. Reichsmarks, rins, roubles, pounds and shekels. It is the international system of currency which determines the totality of life on this planet. That is the natural order of things today.... And you have meddled with the primal forces of nature. And you will atone.

There is no America. There is no democracy. There is only IBM and ITT and AT&T...and DuPont, Dow, Union Carbide and Exxon... The world is a college of corporations...inexorably determined by the immutable by-laws of business. One vast and ecumenical holding company, for whom all men will work to serve a common profit...all necessities provided, all anxieties tranquilized, all boredom amused. And I have chosen you, Mr. Beale, to preach this evangel.

[Beale] Why me?

[Jensen] Because you're on television, dummy; millions of people watch you every night of the week, Monday through Friday.

[Beale] I have seen the face of God.

[Jensen] You just might be right, Mr. Beale.

[pic]

["Network" was brought to Broadway in 2017 and updated technically to comment on new forms of dwindling.]

On Broadway, the at-home TV audience becomes a live audience in the theater; the real audience becomes the audience in the play. That audience is subjected to the new technologies that expand human figures into large screen projections. The new Howard Beale (Bryan Cranston) moves among them with feigned hominess, but his image is gargantuan and shrinks the public into the tight spaces of their seats. While the audience can see the manipulation – the swarm of technicians -- the enhanced image is overwhelming. Jensen's oration has added power, now that, forty years on, we are familiar with our corporate masters and their dominance.

7

"Network" offers a parable here in our time of powerless souls, wandering without political power as their world shatters down upon them, in routines shaped for happy consumers and quiescent citizens. As is typical in so much sci-fi, government slips away to reveal the corporate management that runs things. It is not only "Network", but Spielberg's "AI" or "Ex Machina" or "Blade Runner" where the world is run by business concerns, free to shape the world, while lingering humanity limps along ... . Corporate totalitarianism wields technological marvels and the story-telling prowess that captivates the citizen's hunger for thrills. The sheer boredom of Leisureland excites its residents with flashing shimmer and primal thump of group grope fueled by powerful drugs in their frenzied effort to make this novelty seem new and different. They are not citizens but clients in a humiliating diminishment from which there is no return.

Victims embrace their dwindling willingly. The loss of citizen power to the corporate state is a slow seepage, a coup in slow-motion, scarcely noticed by hard-pressed shoppers and taxpayers, competing for social status and normality. Their loss of unions and free-standing political parties to express social power leaves the denizens of Leisureland unarmed against corporate power. As in Milton's vision, they have become spectators in vast assemblies, within expansive architecture diminishing them. The portals to Leisureland are immense with gleaming glass and metal atriums that awe the senses. Candidates for dwindling tread happily along bright corridors. The excitement is contagious as they fill the stands for a neatly packaged presentations to prospective purchasers of diminished, plastic communities. These future world projections are already familiar to us.

[pic]

[In His Houston Mega-Church, Pastor Joel Osteen guides his shrunken flock.]

Citizenship seeps away, too, in the constant din of television, filling the emptiness with excitements of the news, now the prime entertainment for the middling masses living right at the edge of "not a care in the world". The screens are cleansed of the poor and the sick and the miserable, they focus on the decent middling masses and their consumption styles. The distractions of celebrity and sports provide some ripple of excitement but nothing to awaken awareness of subjection and alarm.

These days, a growing commentary focusses on the decay of democracy into a corporatized spectacle. How can one say that the people have no voice when, at regular intervals they get to choose their leaders? However, in the United States, until recently considered a highly developed democracy, elections offer little choice. The wealthy and powerful dictate the roster of candidates, and, afterwards, the policies and actions of government. The people are aware it is a sham but are distracted by game show personalities to cheer or growl at. This is managed democracy, with its slogans and logos and memes; colorful projections, vivid personalities, and ringing slogans blazoned across the electric web, and dazzling the collective hive in Pandemonium.

PS: "The banks are too big to fail, and we are too small to matter" -- Noam Chomsky

Stephen Zelnick, Professor Emeritus, Temple Univeristy

[i] De Tocqueville quotes Alexander Hamilton from Federalist Paper No. 71 on this theme of the dangers to the people from those who would employ flattery and other wiles: "The republican principle demands, that the deliberative sense of the community should govern the conduct of those to whom they entreat the management of their affairs; but it does not require an unqualified complaisance to every sudden breeze of passion, or to every transient impulse which the people may receive from the arts of men who flatter their prejudices to betray their interests. ... [The people] know from experience that they sometimes err; and wonder is, that they so seldom err as they do, beset, as they continually are, by the wiles of parasites and sycophants; by the snares of the ambitious, the avaricious, the desperate; by the artifices of men who possess their confidence more than they deserve it, and of those who seek to possess rather than deserve it" (Ch. VIII, 154).

[ii] De Tocqueville comments on the dangers of demagogic persuasion in a way that sheds interesting light on the doubloon episode. He writes: "A proposition must be plain to be adopted by the understanding of a people. A false notion which is clear and precise will always have more power in the world than a true principle which is obscure or involved" (Ch. VIII, 166). And further, "mountebanks of all sorts are able to please the people, while their truest friends frequently fail to gain their confidence'" (Ch. XIII, 201). Melville's interest in this issue is intense in "The Confidence-Man" (1857), his last published novel

PART THREE

PART THREE

BREAKDOWNS

Awed Aura

There's an awed aura
after you pass me nude
on the way to our business
of the hour.

You rush ahead
to surprise,
but you surpass.

Tom Sheehan

Editorial by Oonah V Joslin

In honour of James Graham Scottish Poet 1939 to 2019

It was on September 4th 2018 that James Graham and I at last met at his suggestion in Knaresborough, Yorkshire. He and my husband instantly hit it off and went off puffing at their pipes and talking History and politics together. James was in his 80th year and revisiting places he'd known in his youth. On 3rd September 2019, I learned of his death. There's a kind of 'poetic synchronicity' to this opening that James would call 'Nonsense' and in no uncertain tone. This disparity in thinking made unusual friends of us but of course, with us it was always about poetry and language. And it was about being Dalriadan. Ayrshire and Antrim are the same folk. My family undoubtedly hailed from Ayreshire and his father was from Co. Antrim. Many's an online discussion we had about shared dialect, ancestry and history. And we also shared a love of gardens and trees.

I joined Writewords in 2007. The site's poetry expert was, retired teacher, James Graham. Nobody who has not had the benefit of James' in-depth, insightful and gentle commentary on their work can appreciate just how many people James has nurtured over the years or how much he has contributed to their knowledge and skill as poets. Week after week since the site began, James gave serious thought to the work of others and wrote entire swathes of critique. He always printed the poems out so that he could make notes. He questioned, he suggested, he encouraged. He saw each poem through to the end or to its abandonment. His perceptions were frank, honest and useful without ever being unkind, and of course his punctuation was unparalleled. He'd want me to point that out. He was a man of prodigious intellect and an unparalleled knowledge of poetry and literature. He had a passion for History and Art, and he loved meeting people. He said he would have liked to read to a capacity audience at the O2 Arena. I only recorded him reading two of his poems. I wish we had had time to do more.

When James read the following poem and he wrote:
"there's a particular stand of trees at Thorp Perrow arboretum, and I couldn't help noticing that they were all, as far as I could see, practically the same height. As poets you and I both stand tall. No false modesty – I know I've written some good poems, but so have you. So have several other WW members – work that deserves to be far more widely appreciated. I couldn't place us all in ranking order. Poetically we're all handsome silver birches, all 80ft tall, give or take a fraction of an inch."

The Art of Forestry
(for James Graham)

I met you
on your way to
becoming a tree,

at that point
where woodland paths
converge, we met.

You seemed always straight,
tall, rooted in
forest languages,

familiar
with leaf and bark,
versed in mossy soils.

We all grew stronger
under your branches.
Light, filtered through

your determined
shade, greened the sky,
measuring each day's hours by a poem.

And you make sense
of all our knots,
tip us all a wink.

'Time gnarls
everything,' you say,
'but the path always leads to

becoming a tree'.
Heaps of time pile up.
Leaves fall to their deaths.

Words bubble.
But what more could we poets ask?
It's deep in our grain.

I always felt privileged when he liked my work.

James was able to visit Northumberland in Spring 2019 and visit some of my favourite gardens, Wallington, Cragside, Alnwick and Belsay. He loved them all but he said Belsay was best. I was able to introduce him to the work of The Pitmen Painters. We got to celebrate his 80th Birthday ahead of time with mutual friends Tina and Peter Cole who'd come up specially from Hereford.

Of course when you spend time with the 'real someone', you get to know the little things. James was quite infirm by now but fiercely independent. He adored his family and was so proud of his grandchildren. He loved really dark chocolate, cream cakes, ice cream, fish and chips, steak and kidney pie, good traditional food and lots of salt on just about everything. He drank Stella Artois and liked a wee dram. He liked to do jigsaw puzzles.

James was on Writewords and commenting on and writing poems 'til the last. His mind was a sharp as ever. His enthusiasm was undiminished, his kindness unfailing.

There's an archive of his work in Bewildering Stories. I am sure he'd have agreed with their recent FB post:
"Bewildering Stories is a kind of Times Square or Grand Central Station on the Internet. Or, rather, a Heaven."

He was also a regular contributor and great advocate for The Linnet's Wings and Gyroscope Review and many other magazines. James believed that when you're dead, you're dead but his idea of an afterlife resided in his writings. His two books 'Clairvoyance' and 'Becoming a Tree' are available on Amazon and from Troubador Press. They are full of history, humour, sadness and above all beautifully crafted poetry. I cannot recommend them too highly.

If there is a heaven, they'd better get in an eternal supply of pipes and good tobacco because James would consider it hell without them.

For James: At the Duddo Stones

I might have known I'd find you here
your fingers and feet
so gnarled you said
and cold

encircled by ancient human kind
I remember you
who came and are gone
beyond

within this inner land
the turmoil of my billowing dust
you reach out a hand
I know and can trust

your voice fine tuned
calls so quietly I must
respond with all
my being subsumed

beneath the soil
in which my soul is hid
no deeper than this turf
your voice sings down the border wind

that I must pen this infinity of awe
this gift of tears
this cage of fear
with only words

Oonah V Joslin

ART: The King's Wife
Paul Gauguin
Date: 1896; French Polynesia
Style: Cloisonnism
Period: 2nd Tahiti period
Genre: nude painting (nu)
Media: oil, canvas
Location: Pushkin Museum, Moscow, Russia

The Poor Man at his Gate

James Graham

They came, a mass of hodden grey,
to the Thames at Greenwich. They had paid
for Richard's war with France. They had paid
for Windsor Castle, and the Great Chamber's
fur quilts and feather mattresses. They had paid
for the holy golden stuff in many churches.

Enter the King. In ermine cloak, and belt
of winking amethysts and emeralds,
he trod the boards of the Royal Barge.

He raised his voice to bridge
the gulf between and, curious to know,
he asked them what they wanted.
'Come over here on land', one shouted.
The Noble Duke of Salisbury, in goatskin hat,
now intervened. 'You are in no condition',
he bayed, 'to meet the King'. Exit the King.

 As if the windless day had turned to storm,
rage ran like a heavy tide through all the crowd.
'To London!' one voice cried, and 'London! London!'
fell like hail on the departing barge.

They stormed the Marshalsea. Debtors walked free,
and thieves and poachers were as free as kings:

their only victory. At last they came
home to the same four seasons, hunger and the plough,
king and gentry playing the London stage,

the commons not yet sovereign.

ART: Wood with Beech Trees
Piet Mondrian
Date: 1899
Style: Post-Impressionism
Genre: landscape
Media: gouache, watercolor, paper
Location: Gemeentemuseum den Haag, Hague, Netherlands
Dimensions: 45.5 x 57 cm

Summer

James Graham

On a bright day in June
young souls passed through the gates,
released from this life
of vulgar fractions
into a play-eternity,
six weeks in Paradise.

For me, the woods were Heaven.
Some days, it rained, but otherwise
there were trees to climb, or river pools
to capture minnows in a jar
and pour them back, or paths to follow
to a sacred rock where I would sit
believing myself wise,
or to the cave where I
put on my hermit's cloak
and prophesied. I alone
in all the world, knew of this place.

Sometimes young spirits from the village
would meet me at the apple orchard,
climb the wall and take
the forbidden fruit. Old Mister God
must have been elsewhere
for he never thundered, and we
were not cast out. We never knew
what time it was, for this
was everlasting life. And I would show
them my timeless woods (but not the cave),
the pretty cows, the rabbit-holes,
and the birds' nests in the hedgerows.

Then home to tea.

ART:Fee-fi-fo-fum, I smell the blood of an Englishman

Arthur Rackham

Style: Art Nouveau (Modern)

Series: English Fairy Tales

Genre: illustration

Alien

James Graham

I met an alien
and I could not understand him.

He wore jeans and a white sweatshirt.
He had two eyes, two ears,
his cheek was shaven, rather pale.
Perhaps his brain was green, his soul
small-mouthed, large-eyed.

He spoke English, but the gist of it was cloud.

He jabbered about blacks and Jews. His face
became buckled, his eyes bloated.
But I cannot report his words.

I do not understand. I have had
no feelings such as I could recognise
from any syllable of his speaking.

Transformation: River to Oxbow Lake

Ceinwen E C Haydon

Once, my urgent, pulsing flow
pressed at loam sidings,
softened clay mudflats
and swirled around bends.
My wild currents
built breaking waves
to come repeatedly crashing
out through brackish marshland,
oyster beds, and on into the sea.

In this calmer time
sand and stony soil, outcropped,
form barriers and grassy mounds,
dry ground to stem my flow.
I am paused, landlocked,
my damp comma settling still
among grazed fields.
Only my calm surface moves,
ruffled to Chantilly lace
in gentle winds.

Yet I dream, in moonlight,
of floods. Lunar magnets
whose forces flicker freely
between firmament and earth.
Dream of a night-time deluge
with the might to merge us,
wee oxbow lakes, to waterways
with lustful surges, strong enough
to break our banks and
shudder pleasure in surrender.

Like Chalk Erased From The Sidewalk

Akeith Walters

So, let's speak
about
what we've unspoken too much,

love's
ethereal memory
made tangible

in the accidental
of a toddler's handprint in wet walkway cement
worn smooth

grey
under years of absent steps
where ferns overgrow around

until found
in the happenstance glance at the back of a hand
that's come to visit,

age-spotted
as it reaches out to push the fronds aside

to help
in a step-up

to the heart's front door that (has been)
(is)
(will)

always open for you, my child.

Spider
Theodor Severin Kittelsen
Style: Realism
Genre: sketch and study

It Frays

Caroline Hardaker

The arachnid trickles across the silk pillow like blood
might run, like licking,

as a frown moves down a face. Hooks, etched from
sable,

hawk into thatched threads – tickled to fray, and

click, click, click go the coiling thorns,

mounted in preparation for a strike. A brush of air on
these palps

and the giant raises on iron arches to bare a copious
nut-belly –

a fortified conker bristling with arrows,

primed to prick their fire through the skin of plums, ripe
to suckle on.

It is Goliath, the cotton weave his cobweb.

Then, tissued away
released onto a landing leaf, softly softly,

it withers,

curling shy of sunlight.

John C. Mannone

Let Me Count Thirteen Ways on How I Love You

After Elizabeth Barrett Browning & Wallace Stevens

1
Fresh ground coffee and buttered toast
Mushroom & rosemary frittata
Served on a cobalt blue plate
    I never leave you hungry

2
We cook and wash together
I glance at you under kitchen sunlight
Your hair coppery
    Your smile seductive
    Even without makeup

3
A walk through the Garden
Before we are caught
In the rain
    Your eyes glistening

4
Making *love*-
-*Related* poetry with you
Trading words...looks
    Cuddling in the candlelight
    Tucking you in

5

Throwing the sheer cotton
Curtains aside
Sliding the glass door open
  To thunder-rain
  Lightning dancing
  In your eyes

6

I give you all, all of me
And you give me all, all of you
Is not just a love song
  It's morning dew
  On a blade of grass in the fall

7

I bring you
Flurries and *Hurricanes* and *Blizzards*
Yet you stay
  I love you more than popcorn

8

Counting fireflies
Spring meteors flashing sky
Driving under moonlight
  For midnight pancakes

9

You can drive
You can sit at the end of the isle
You can be late
  And I will still be happy
  Even if I'm crying

10
Playing word games and sipping wine
Savoring Walker shortbread cookies
With you in our pajamas
      Until three in the morning

11

Holding the door open
To my heart
Letting you walk in
      All the way

12
Caressing
Your hands your palms
Our fingers
      Reading Braille
      Of unspoken words

13
And of course our kisses
Which make supernovas
Seem like mere fire-
      -Crackers

ART: The Gardner, Giuseppe Arcimboldo, Date:
c.1590, Style: Mannerism (Late Renaissance),
Series: Visual Pun,
Genre: allegorical painting,Media: oil, wood,
Location: Museo Civico Ala Ponzone, Cremona,
Italy

I Used to Be Immortal

Irena Pasvinter

I used to be immortal, long ago,
When endless years lay ahead in waiting
And none of my beloved had to go.

When grandpa left, it was a deadly blow
But just a hint of what was still awaiting:
I used to be immortal, long ago.

Then grandma went. I had my kids to grow...
After a while the pain began abating,
Though some of my beloved had to go.

But dad... Tell, God, why did he have to go
So early? You're deaf -- no use debating.
Dad used to be immortal, long ago.

And you, my mom, swept by the mortal blow
Of cruel fate that shrewdly lay in waiting
When none of my beloved had to go.

And now, at last, I'm mortal and I know
That death is dozing somewhere, awaiting.
I used to be immortal, long ago,
When none of my beloved had to go.

ART: Death and Life, Gustav Klimt, Date: 1908 -
1916, Style: Art Nouveau (Modern),
Period: Golden phase, Genre: allegorical painting,
Media: oil, canvas

Scones And Jam

Dolores Duggan

The radio droned in the corner.
Some old talk show.
As you boiled the kettle
To make a pot of tea.
It spilled onto the range
You cursed as you mopped it up.
Tea and scones, real butter and jam
And whipped cream.
You preferred honey but
The bees weren't playing ball this summer.
Early days you said we will have plenty
Enough to keep the winter away.
Blue Tits chirped outside the window.
We threw crumbs for them and
Watched and waited as we sipped
Our tea on that balmy day.
Till later, when the sun went down.

ART: The Butterfly Hunter, Carl
Spitzweg, Original Title: Der
Schmetterlingsjäger, Date: 1840;
Germany, Style: Biedermeier, Genre:
genre painting, Media: oil, panel

Being Present

Anne Donnellan

Humanity
Beaming across cosmic screens
Suspended reality transposed to fantasy
As a compassionless cloud envelopes our being
And indifference triumphs as never before
No protest
No placards
No pressure no more

Knowledge trumps conscience
With every smart gadget
Awareness is deadened
As all in the gallery are subservient and silenced
That we did not know never let us plead
A defense of the past for heinious deeds
Complicity compounded through mega connectivity
With super sensitive sensors
And distant control actors
Being present is paramount
Intent assumed
Collective culpability
Forever presumed.

ART: Descent of the Holy Ghost upon the
Faithful, Jean Fouquet,
Original Title: Le Dextre de Dieu chassant les
Démons,
Date: 1452 - 1460,
Style: Northern Renaissance,
Series: Hours of Etienne Chevalier,
Genre: religious painting

Bird Breveament

Alisa Velaj

Last midnight, our goldfinch passed away.
My father was overwhelmed with sorrow
as I'd hardly ever seen him before.
Morning was slow to come,
with a lonely canary in the other cage,
now facing the empty one in front.
Oh, how long we waited for our canary to sing!
We waited and waited the whole day out...
Still, voice-locked, she suddenly died in the evening.

My grief then grew fathomless,
for I was reminded of a night of nights,
when the news reported of a violated pedestrian,
while we sat to dine as usual,
mindless even of a prayer for the poor soul.
[We only commented that, in this country,
one's life is worth less than a feather].

Our frail canary, instead, sang no more upon losing her friend...

Translated from Albanian: ARBEN P. LATIFI

ART:Cleopatra, preparatory study
for 'Cleopatra Testing Poisons on
the Condemned Prisoners'
Alexandre Cabanel
Style: Academicism
Genre: history painting
Media: oil, canvas

ART: Patcher breaks sign (Barin at the house of patcher)
Boris Kustodiev
Original Title: Штопальщик срывает вывеску (Барин у дома штопальщика)
Date: 1922
Style: Realism
Series: Nikolay Leskov "Patcher"
Genre: literary painting

The March of Time

Lesley Timms

Creeping over kitchen walls,
inquisitive sunlight unveils a calendar.
March, bright, laden with
boldly-penned plans.

Glinting now on laid out
breakfast spoon, cup, bowl,
curiously undisturbed today.

Revealing a hard-faced clock,
relentless ticks hammering each second
into the irretrievable past.

Shining down on the open TV guide,
reflecting upon this evening's
heavily-circled programmes.

Lighting upon faded pink slippers
faithful by the back door, still waiting
to soften her faltering step.

But longed-for splashes of
amethyst and gold will dazzle
unadmired in glistening snow;
familiar blackbirds go unfed.

The Geese Fly North

Nick Bowman

Overhead, a ragged wishbone heads North
to Spring quarters. Wings lever against fat bodies,
bird bone and feather crave the horizon.
On the downbeats they call to each other,
wheezing like ancient bagpipes monotone as dark sky,
they fly over the hill's edge,
disappear like a magician's trick.

At the gate she watches them.
And now with a hiss of salt wind
on this stubborn, stillborn day
she is, for a moment, the most solitary person.
Standing alone, she strains to hear the voices
of all the people she has known,
the strands that joined them fade like breath.
She turns away, decides on a walk to the village
to buy conversation at the shops.

The geese, she would say, are the slow hand of the year,
a reminder of her own flock
that she loved to swaddle against the cold.
But they too flew North leaving time in their place.

On some days she opens all the windows,
cocks her head like a bird to listen.
News of their losses and victories seeps in
as she sleeps in the afternoons.
Sometimes she wakes and is twenty five again,
for a few seconds at least,
her goslings around her feet.

ART Peasant Woman Watching
the Geese
Camille Pissarro
Date: 1890
Style: Impressionism
Genre: genre painting
Media: oil, canvas
Location: Private Collection

As Autumn comes she scans the hilltop,
longs for rain and sleet and the
shortening days that unknot her heart.
When they come, they take apart
the long summer piece by piece,
filling the air with noise.
Their return turns back a lifetime
as if it was yesterday.

Mother Moon

Ann Thornfield-Long

Since ancient times,
we have called you

by your secret names:
worm moon when earth

thaws, hunger moon in the last
lean month of winter.

Like cats we mark you
as our own with scent and blood

of mortals. You bring us
menstruation and tears. Women

want to walk your sharp
and glistening shores.

When you shine across
still water, we fall

in love. With whispers
you call children

to our wombs. We will
bathe your daughters

in the platinum light
of your unblinking eye.

She-wolves, we will sing
your secret names to stars.

ART: The Wolves Descending from the Alps
William Hamilton
Date: 1794
Style: Neoclassicism
Genre: genre painting

Murmurration

Mathew Paust

Murmur, my ass
clearly more cackle...no
not that, either...tinkle
tinkle...Yes!

A myriadation of tintinnabulation
a cacophonous eruption
from the marshes in the south
an interminable, chittering gush over Court House Main

Swirling into the town's winter trees
filling bone-bare branches for a moment's break
its iridescence lost in silhouette against a near-dawn sky, the teeming, treble-voices
socializing, confabulating whither to next?

ART: The Goulue and Valentin, The Boneless One
Henri de Toulouse-Lautrec
Original Title: Le Goulue and Valentin, the Boneless One
Date: 1891
Style: Art Nouveau (Modern)
Genre: genre painting
Location: Musee Toulouse-Lautrec, Albi, France

Moon Dance, Trees Coming Green, April

Tom Sheehan

Shadows leap out of themselves. The moon has crooked legs and trips and stumbles into corners not ready for lighting up, and forks of trees, alleys, an edge of the pond coming slack from ice.I walk the unthickening pond in its whole perimeter, walk off a bad letter and poems returned in my writing from a far editor's desk, a case of hives burning on my arms and sending false rumors into my groin.I feel volcanic, that I will come to ash and nothing else, that I burn here and come down slowly to ash— the lava of my life creeping away from me, spending itself.But there is the moon dancing St. Elmo's fire on maple limbs struggling out of the iron winter, breaking out of chained skin, leaping ahead of me the whole way myriad as a street-long web.

But there is the moon laying my shadow on asphalt proving me taller than I am. I spin my arms of shadows into the wake of the moon and this propeller drives me on past my own house again this night. Twice I have gone by and have not gone into its whispers, those calibres of sounds

I can measure almost in sleep:
the hums of refrigeration, the crackling
laughter of a late fire so late this time
of year, wife who sighs before she shifts
into deep blankets' recess; sons, daughters,
twisting overhead, spilling their dreams for
me so that I can climb into the light burning
in their night lives, candlepower of thought,
love galleons from Matthew's soiled pages—
triceratops, dyplodicus, king rex, those "walking houses" he dreams after reading.

He is awed at the ponderous, the gigantic, room-filling images, and James falls into his footprints, leans to the gargantuan, wears the creatures in his eyes, thick of armor, earth-moving.
But now the moon falls as flakes into their room through screening— porous moon fall, chips of light, afghans of pawns and pieces, a tapestry of dreaming sons. Their arms and legs are rivers to and from the lakes of their hearts, these growing waters, these floods, these dream bones stretching in tides, these pounding waves of muscles, cascade of sons in the moondance, these things beginning in me.
And I go to my beginning and walk past the house again shedding my armor, coring down to each breath, each bubble my mouth takes and gives back; then holding one breath as prisoner, marking it deeply inside, feel its nails clawing to get out as if some bomb would burst in that inner cannister.

But it is the moon that explodes in the field without trees,
a not so golden fire, a splurge of yellow cream, ochre burst finding me in idolatry of this portion of the year.
What burns is all the inner core, all the touched existences, all these images broken in the midnight's press, the earth letting go, my accepting such release.

ART: Shadows. Moonlit Night. by Isaac Levitan
Original Title: Тени. Лунная ночь.
Date: c.1885; Russian Federation
Style: Realism
Genre: landscape
Media: watercolor, paper
Location: National Gallery of Armenia, Yerevan, Armenia

Evening - The End of the Day (after Millet)
by Vincent van Gogh

A Balmy Day
James G Piatt

I listen to the color of emptiness in the fading hours that cover the vanishing images of a common day. My feelings descend into a metaphoric translucent pond; nostalgic ripples travel to the edges where green frogs are croaking at the sun. My thoughts wade through the absurdity of silence, watching tall reeds swaying to the pulse of the balmy day's waning moments.

The fragrance of earthy loam enters my senses as I weave dreams out of vines covering the edge of the pond. A sudden hush rests upon my mind as the frailty of the season settles into the wet soil, sprouting colorful flowers, redefining reality. I feel the soft touch of the balmy spring breeze; it circles then touches my weary body after it curves around the edge of the sun, beaming warmth to the earth.

Offeren y Llwyn:
Dafydd ap Gwilym

Lle digrif y bûm heddiw
dan fentyll y gwyrddgyll gwiw
yn gwarando ddechrau dydd
y ceiliog bronfraith celfydd
yn canu englyn alathr,
arwiddion y llithion llathr.

Pellennig, pwyll ei annwyd,
pell ei siwrnail'r llatai llwyd.
Yma y doeth o swydd goeth Gaer
am ei erchi o'm eurchwaer,
geiriog, heb yn gair gwarant,
sef y cyrch i Nentyrch nant.

Morfudd a'i hanfanasai,
mydr ganiadaeth mab maeth Mai.

ART
Passing Summer
Willard Metcalf
Date: 1916
Style: Impressionism
Genre: landscape
Location: Private Collection
Dimensions: 91.44 x 91.44 cm

Amdano yr oedd gasmai
o flodau mwyn gangau Mai,
a'i gasul, debygesynt,
o esgyll, gwyrdd fentyll, gwynt.

Nid oedd yna, myn Duw mawr,
Ond aur oll yn do'r allawr.
Mi a glywwn mewn gloywiaith
ddatganu, nid methu, maith,
darllain i'r plwyf, nid rhwyf rhus,
efengyl yn ddifyngus.

Codi ar fryn ynn yna
afrlladen o ddeilen dda.
Ac eos gain fain fangaw
o gwr y llwyn gar ei llaw,
clerwraig nant, i gant a gan
cloch aberth, clau ei chwiban,
a dyrchafel yr aberth
hyd y nen uwchben y berth:
a chrefydd i'n Dafydd Dad
a charegl nwyf a chariad.

Bodlon wyfi'r ganiadaeth,
bedwlwyn o'r coed mwyn a'i maeth.

The Woodland Mass

Translation

by Thomas Norman

Lovely is this place where I would stay
listening at the quiet dawn of day
'neath mantles of fine green hazel
upon the bold cock-thrush's skill,
singing a stanza on wings of love,
fluent with signs and symbols from above.

Wisdom his nature our visiting stranger.
Journeyed far this sleek grey messenger,
bringing tidings from fair Carmarthenshire,
requested by my golden haired lover.

Eloquent, but with no warranty,
he came, into our peaceful valley.

Morfudd sent him; my true lover,
fosterson of May, artful songster
garlanded about with branches so gay,
vestments of the sweetly flowering may.
Around his chausable, winged as the wind,
mantles there were close entwined.

Nothing was there; except the Lord God,
but the alter with its canopy of gold.
Hearing in language most pure and clear
ceaseless chanting so pleasant to hear,
distinct, a reading to the people,
memorable voice of the perfect gospel.

Raised upon a mound there to offer
communion's good leaf, the Holy Wafer.
Then did proclaim the slim nightingale,
singing to the many; Poetess of the vale,
whistling lively the Sanctus Bell,
nearby from a thicket the sweet notes fell.

Lifting the Holy Sacrifice up high,
above the bush, to the vaulted sky,
devotion to the Lord our Father.
Ecstasy brimmed the chalice for my lover.

Content now am I with the song of love,
nurtured in this sweet woodland grove.

ART
Succession, Wassily Kandinsky, Date: 1935, Style: Abstract Art, Genre: abstract, Media: oil,
Location: Philips Collection, Washington, DC, US, Dimensions: 100 x 81 cm